Into the F[...]
of Transformation

I Ray

in gRattude

and

with Lou

Donald

Into the Foothills
of Transformation

Donald Eadie

wild goose
publications www.**ionabooks**.com

This book is dedicated to my wife Kerstin, our daughters Nicola and Annika and their families.

'So to claim back the night is to claim darkness as a time for growth and transformation. It is to free darkness of its overtones of evil and sin and see it as potential richness, fertility, hidden growth and contemplation, as nature broods and contemplates in winter, seemingly inactive, yet preparing for the birthing of spring. It is in darkness that new vision is born ... But just as the "work of winter" is indispensable, so the period of darkness has its own tools and activity. Although there is no comfort and even no real hope experienced for the future, and memories of the past bring no security, the process demands that we move forward, with anger, rage and grief our tools, the solidarity of support groups our resource, trust in the absent God our guide – to an alternative we have no name for, only yearning.'

– Mary Grey in *Redeeming the Dream*, SPCK, 1989

Contents

In gratitude

I am grateful to Neil Paynter, editor at Wild Goose Publications, for his invitation, in December 2015, to share with him reflections and meditations written over the years: '*I like a journey and discovering threads … I imagine some of those pieces will "just" need careful copy-editing, tidying, proofing, and some might need a little development, shaping …*'

In the spring and summer of 2016 I experienced debilitating pain and a loss of confidence and energy. It was in the late autumn that I began working on both the completed and almost completed writing, seeking the threads, a possible shape, an overall theme and title. It has been, and remains, a work in process. I wrote to Neil, '*I seek your wisdom to transform this writing into becoming more accessible and helpful.*' Above all he has encouraged me to work with what is emerging. His invitation has felt providential and I am profoundly grateful to him personally and to members of the Iona Community.

I am also grateful to Peter Whale, Peter Cole and Valerie Edden who saw more in the writing than first I recognised, encouraged me to 'stay with it', and advised on what would make the text more readable. Valerie knew when the time had come to 'hand it over', and more recently to 'let go' of the book permitting it to travel where it will.

Joanna Burnett has been a soul friend with the writing on adoption; she inhabits the dark, silent and lonely corridors of the adoption journey with such humility and wisdom.

Bernie Arscott and Merlin Young know the mystery of the human body and have become more than mentors: they are trusted companions.

Jane Walton has read and critiqued the body section of the book with shrewd wisdom and is much more than a retired senior nurse.

Neil Richardson is a former colleague and a friend, a New Testament scholar and a man in the world.

Ursula and John Turner are our oldest shared friends, still waiting for me to write about 'life' in ways they can understand. So I will watch their furrowed brows, and hopefully, their creasing smiles.

Most of all I am grateful to my family, who have accompanied me through so much that I have written about. They have read and re-read different sections of the book, encouraging and challenging me – especially my language!

There is one more person. In June 2013 Father Stan accompanied me in an eight-day silent retreat at St Beuno's Jesuit Spirituality Centre near St Asaph in North Wales. He urged me to write about the new life I am discovering.

Note:

John Turner died in September 2018.

Introduction

Increasingly I wonder about the nature of transformation and those transformative encounters that bring us to a place of wonder, gazing and trembling. It is within these foothills that I invite the reader to explore. It is my hope that all kinds of people will find enough resonances within their humanity to bring them to smile in recognition.

In my book *Grain in Winter* I wrote of our learning to wait within the 'in-between times', and what sustains us during periods of bewildering and messy transitions. It was written for those of us who face change in our lives but do not know what that change might entail nor where it may lead. The writing emerged during three long periods of convalescence following spinal operations in the 1990s. The new life that emerged was different to anything I could have planned or would have chosen and had implications for our family in ways we could not have anticipated. I am learning that sometimes within our loss and grieving, disappointments and rage, fears and tears there is a loosening, a cracking open and a fresh flowing of life, a freedom permitting a deeper yet hidden realignment, and a joyful inner homecoming. These experiences are essentially intermingling, not to be held as separate. I have struggled to find these words and hope they may resonate.

I find this same paradox resonating within Christian tradition and in particular in the life, the death that leads to entombment, and the resurrection of Jesus of Nazareth. We cannot box these transitions into three separate religious compartments; to do so is to miss what is essentially all intertwined within life's wonder and perplexity.

I want to explore these transforming encounters within a wide variety of thresholds, including the basement of a textile factory; the experience of being adopted; a classroom of children; living with a body which knows both pleasure and pain; the arrival of asylum seekers in a small Swedish village; taking off our shoes in our local mosque … I describe these encounters in what some describe as 'Donald language', namely 'third-day resonances'.

In recent years there have been two further periods in hospital. One for a bypass operation in my left leg leading to a fasciotomy, a surgical procedure resulting in a long wound that remained open for nearly four months, attended to daily by district nurses. The other was an unexpected and bewildering period in hospital after becoming delirious during a bout of pneumonia. It was within these scary terrains that life cracked open. Writing became one of my ways of accepting and integrating what was going on around and within me. At times it has become so necessary – as if something wants to be born from the almost indecipherable jottings scribbled in the middle of the night, or while waiting in an outpatient clinic or lying in a hospital ward. On occasions these were formed into letters, articles and addresses.

Within what I have written there is an old mantra, *'Thou, O Lord, art in our midst.'* It belongs to my soul breathing and has accompanied me however I am feeling – in the heights and in the depths and wherever I am. It has developed through the years into *'Thou, O Lord, art in our midst, life-giver, truth-revealer and compassionate One.'* This has become my heart prayer.

Who is this writing for? It is for those living with curiosity, those given to gazing, wondering, pondering, those who are open to the place of trembling. It is for those with enough humility to be open to differences in world view, in spoken language, in religious culture; open to being transformed through these encounters. It is for those learning to be attentive in entering the depths of our humanity; learning to let go and trust within our yielding into the unknown; those who hesitantly open themselves to the way of transformative love in a world living through a 'global nervous breakdown'.

Among those who are closest to me, who challenge and inspire me, are those for whom 'religious words get in the way', some of whom have thoughtfully read and responded to earlier drafts of my writing. They urge that I do not airbrush out the language of God and faith: 'it belongs within its authenticity even if it does not hold meaning for us'. They are among those who show us what kneeling, hearkening and seeing could mean in our troubled world and where daring to live our faithfulness might lead.

Those who read this book will become aware of my wife, Kerstin, what she has lived through and continues to live through. Kerstin has read much of what has been written, she has encouraged me when I have felt low and near to giving up. She experiences the writing as intensely moving yet has lived these stories from a different perspective. Her life has been reshaped and the direction has not been one of her choosing. Kerstin continues to carry so much both physically and emotionally that makes our life together and also our life with others possible – and much more than possible, rich and good.

This introduction was written as we approach Easter 2018. I am waiting for a triple heart bypass, thankful for the possibility of a new life but a bit scared about the process.

The foothills
of transformation

Into the foothills of transformation

'It is as if I am inhabiting paradox for the first time. The place of contraction and limitation has become the place of expansion and deepening: I am discovering solidarity within solitude, availability for others within my new stability, being at the heart of things while living on the edge. There has been a freedom to enter silence, to cherish the body that is in pain and to learn to love myself during a time when self-image has been badly bruised and broken. There has been an inner homecoming.'

From my journal

The mystery of transformation lies, I believe, within the heart of everything and it is not easy to find the words we seek. My starting place has been our encounter with 'the mystery of things' within the ordinariness of things, awakening wonder and more – a following where wondering may lead.

I wonder about those encounters we sometimes describe as transformative. What is it that permits us, within our vulnerability, to let go control and yield into a future we cannot imagine?

I am learning that the agonising process of transformation is the very nature of God's engagement within our humanity. Some ask, 'Agonising, does it have to be agonising?'

My way into this exploration begins in the foothills.

The metamorphic process

I have seen red-hot lava spewing out of the great depths of a volcano. I tremble in the place of 'meltdown' and wonder what it might mean for us.

I rarely use the word 'metamorphic' but have discovered it can help in our understanding of the nature of transformation. Years ago a South African nun shared with me a dream she had in which she discovered she was holding a diamond. In our time together she wanted to reflect on the metamorphic processes that take place deep within the earth under great pressure and heat and which produce diamonds.

I have a close friend, John, who knows about these things; he draws me into the mystery of galaxies beyond galaxies, the migration patterns of birds, their long journeys at times asleep on the wing. I wrote to him about the metamorphic process and he replied:

> 'A short geology course is needed: you will know (I imagine) that some of the rocks we see have spent part of their lives at depths of several miles. Diamonds and kimberlite, the rock in which diamonds usually occur, are formed in the plumbing of ancient volcanoes as a result of the pressures and temperatures they have been subjected to. The process is called metamorphosis. There are many forms of metamorphic rock. Slate is metamorphosed shale; marble is metamorphosed limestone. The east coast of Sweden is composed of metaphoric rock, as is much of Scotland. The common feature of all this is the pressure and temperature caused by deep burial.'

John and I have been friends for over 60 years, and have shared the heights and depths in our different experiences of life. He helps me to make unexpected connections; smiles on my wondering about the nature of transformation in human communities and in our being human.

The chrysalis

There are many images of transformation.

Jean is a 91-year-old friend much given to gazing and pondering.

She wrote:

> 'The butterfly is my symbol of transformation. The caterpillar
> is totally different from the adult, flying butterfly. In between,
> contained in the hard case of the chrysalis, the tissues of the
> body are completely broken down and re-formed. As you know,
> and as I have noted before to you, the ancient Greek for but-
> terfly, psyche (with all that means), translates as soul …
>
> The frog is another symbol. Its life is gradual: the tadpole
> grows, loses its tail, hops from the water to the land as a tiny
> frog and grows to maturity. This is known as incomplete meta-
> morphosis (the butterfly is complete).'

I wonder what the notion of 'incomplete' and 'complete' transformation might mean for us and upon what the complete transition
depends.

Someone once told me that for years she had felt shrivelled up as
one who had died, but was now crawling out of her dead chrysalis
like a butterfly learning to fly – as if for the first time. She is not
alone in this scary journey.

A dragonfly story:

Two caterpillars on a warm summer's day looked up and saw a
dragonfly dipping over a pond. One said to the other: 'You
wouldn't get me up in a thing like that!'

Morphing

Two of our friends, both of whom are retired head teachers, came
for coffee one morning and during our conversation spoke of
'morphing': a classroom of unruly children being 'morphed', a
staffroom of exhausted, fractious teachers being 'morphed'. When
asked about these encounters with morphing they spoke of a
dynamic within the chemistry of a classroom, within a staffroom:
a transformative process.

I had not been aware of the word 'morphing' in common parlance (I live a sheltered life). An invitation to live through these messy mysteries belongs to all of us.

During my three periods in hospital our ward had the same senior nurse, who was from northern Borneo. On occasions when hidden tensions were about to burst in the ward he chose to stand conspicuously still in a place where all could see and hear. His custom was to tell parables drawn from his own culture but that could be understood by all of us and at many levels. The nurses, doctors, cleaners and patients all stopped what they were doing and listened. He addressed us in a direct yet whimsical way, gently and with a light touch, without judgement, somehow diffusing situations with the potential for eruption, transforming the dynamics of the ward, and leaving us all with life questions to ponder. 'This is how he runs the ward,' a nurse said to me.

Hula Hoops?*

I was asked to lead a Quiet day and chose 'transformation' as our theme. People had been invited to bring their symbols of encounters with that mystery we call transformation, and early on in the day to lay them on a table in the centre of our circle. During the periods of quiet, people walked around the table looking with an attentive interest which seemed more than curiosity.

At the conclusion of the day I reminded people to collect their symbols before going home. An older person broke the quietness in a way that may have surprised some. 'I am moved by so many of the symbols of transformation, but cannot understand why anyone can place a bag of Hula Hoops among them. Would the person who brought it please explain?'

---

* *A kind of crisp sold in the UK*

It could have been a violating moment but mercifully wasn't. Present was a young Afro-Caribbean woman who had severe problems with her sight; she was accompanied by an older white woman. She stood up and quietly, yet with confidence, humour and utter authenticity, told her story:

'When I was a teenager I was very rebellious, kicked against everything and everyone. I was sent to an institution where I continued to kick against everything and everyone ... Then one day a member of staff asked if I would be willing to be in charge of the tuck shop: sweets, crisps, Hula Hoops, and also the money. And I accepted. For the first time in my life I learned that someone trusted me. And that was my turning point and the beginning of my transformation.'

There was hardly a dry eye: she had understood.

Another hospital wondering

During one period in hospital, I caught a glimpse of something I find hard to express:

What is it deep down within us that permits those territories of human experience that frighten us – the dark, negative and destructive – to be not only recognised and owned but somehow mysteriously transformed? The reality may not be removed; however it becomes the context for deepening and growing. Why it happens to some and not for others remains a mystery. This is true for both individuals and communities. For a moment I became aware of what transformation can be.

Healing, a journey into a deeper wholeness

'We want to get you back to the work you love,' the surgeon said during the period of my three spinal operations. But this did not happen.

Later the same surgeon helped me to accept my physical reality. 'This is it,' he said, 'you have lots of living to live – get on with it. Don't lose yourself down the plughole of self-pity.' Some of us need help to accept our physical situation, and help with strategies to manage what at times feels unmanageable.

But I am learning a healing deeper than the physical one we wanted and prayed for. When, before early retirement, I was offered a sabbatical, my mentor asked: 'What is your heart's deepest desire?' I knew immediately: search for my birth parents. I am adopted, and learned later the significance of emotional healing. I am grateful to those who helped me face the fears and fantasies, made journeys to search records and registers, the Barnardo's social worker who opened my 'fat file' and compassionately gave me my birth names and fragments of my story. I am thankful to my adopting parents and brother who loved me into being, to my wife and daughters who also love me and who have explored the back corridors of my life story with me.

Our 'yes' to the way of transformation

I wonder about those thresholds in life where we tremble, encounter both fear and promise, and face choices. Our 'yes' could draw us deeply into ways that could become transformative.

In 2002 we received an invitation to attend the Methodist Conference in Sri Lanka. My response was an intuitive 'yes', though for some who know and love us our 'yes' to entering such unfamiliar terrains while living with my physical limitation was a surprising one.

The President of the Sri Lankan Methodist Conference, Noel Fernando, was, I discovered, a quiet, modest, courageous man. Sri Lanka had lived with the trauma of civil war for too many years and it was within this context that he made the recommendation that Tamil and Sinhalese members of the conference should meet not as in the past in Colombo, but in Kalmunai, in the eastern province. This carried a significance we were only slowly to comprehend. The long journey to the east coast would involve travelling through many military checkpoints and into areas dominated by the Tamil national resistance movement, known to us in the West as the Tamil Tigers. This recommendation by the President was all the more remarkable because it was made months before the ceasefire and was met with considerable resistance.

The 'yes' to this first historic journey saw Tamils and Sinhalese travelling on motorbikes, in cars, vans and buses over the mountains toward the eastern coast.

The opening day of the conference began with a procession through the dusty streets. Tamils and Sinhalese walked side by side, singing together. The people of Kalmunai who watched must have wondered what was happening. What was the meaning of this unusual event? That day became a prophetic sign, a glimpse of transformation.

Following into the 'yes'

A friend who came to see me began by finding her tissues, smiling and saying, 'I'm probably going to cry a lot.' In recent years she has experienced much loss. To my surprise, and also her own, within the breakdowns, within the breaking open, there has been a *breaking through*, a following within the unfolding, an emerging.

She told me how she had given her 'yes' to opportunities she would previously not even have considered: 'Yes' to a school cycling tour in Europe in the summer; 'yes' to a class on cycle maintenance; 'yes' to a working week in Mumbai, and to a school trip to the Lake District; 'yes' to concerts and to the theatre, sometimes on her own; 'yes' to the reclaiming of music, her own preferences not other people's choices, and to signing up for dance classes; 'yes' to a holiday in Wales on her own – simply walking all day out in the open air, absorbing all the beauty, bird-watching, strolling the length of beaches, kicking up the waves in the sea, watching the sunset, getting in each night exhausted and ready to sleep …

The liminal place

I am learning about 'the liminal place', the name given by some to describe the rugged terrain we must traverse as communities and also as individual pilgrims.

It describes the 'in-between times' within which we live, the incompleteness of things, the unresolvedness, including the desolation within our experience of our loss of identity, direction, control, clarity.

Others describe these rugged terrains as 'the end times': periods of profound transition within familiar institutions and organisations (religious, educational and social), and our need to help them die well. And more: the importance of our waiting and watching for the unfolding, the emerging of new patterns and forms belonging to what some call 'resurrection'. To have faith is to trust enough to let go and follow within what is unfolding, emerging …

'And he made of the abyss a road'

Norwyn Denny was my senior colleague and friend in the Ecumenical Team Ministry in Notting Hill. In his latter years he wrote a remarkable paper exploring the testimony to Jesus as one who '*descended into hell*'. It followed Norwyn's own serious illness and surgery. He wrote:

> '*The abyss, the desperate experience, the descent into anguish of any kind, is something that comes to most of us at some time or another. Reflection on the abyss sparked off the reaching out*

for meaning in such times and some understanding through them ... I would like to say that, in my own petty experience, what for me was a picture and a feeling of hell, was also for me an experience of the presence of God. God is in hell, to rescue people like you and me within and from this experience, here and hereafter. I believe this because I believe that Jesus "descended into hell" for this very purpose. It underlines strongly for me the belief that God does not forsake us, and that God, in Christ, comes to redeem the very hell that we, or others, make or experience, or will experience ... And he made of the abyss a road. Because of the sacrifice and commitment of Christ, the place of utter despair, terror, pain and evil becomes a road to bring us nearer God.' [1]

Following into the way of transformation

I am still learning what our 'yes' to the way of transformative love might mean and where it could lead us.

Barbara Glasson writes most poignantly about these things, so much so that reading these words out loud can bring me to tears:

'To be followers of Jesus is to go to the depths of who we are, into the soup of metamorphosis, into the possibility that we might be consumed, destroyed, annihilated. To risk finding God, we must lose everything, and I mean everything, even God.' [2]

'... the liminal threshold is messy and full of confusion and contradiction. It is this very messiness that is the medium for re-creation. It is a troubling place, a place where the waters are disturbed and the self becomes immersed into new dimensions of being.' [3]

'And crucially this process holds the potential to bring about transformation not just for the individuals concerned but also

for communities who would take the risk of entering the liminal space and accompany the transitional person across the threshold into new life.' [4]

I scarcely know what this might mean but am learning that our 'Amen' to the bread broken, the wine poured out can become our 'yes' to being drawn into these mysteries, into becoming human in the way Jesus was human.

'... in Jesus we find the agonising process of transformation to be the very nature of God's engagement with humanity.' [5]

A short prayer for a long journey:

Bring us to the Third Day.

Walter Brueggemann

Notes:

1. Norwyn Denny, from *The Descent into Hell*, an unpublished paper. Used by permission of Julia Creese.

2. From *The Exuberant Church: Listening to the Prophetic People of God*, Barbara Glasson, Darton, Longman & Todd, London, 2011, p.44. Used by permission of the publishers

3. ibid. p.97. Used by permission of Darton, Longman & Todd

4. ibid. p.102. Used by permission of Darton, Longman & Todd

5. ibid. p.44. Used by permission of Darton, Longman & Todd

Echoes of an inner yet cosmic music

I wonder about music: where it comes from and its echoes within the process of transformation.

Within everything we begin to listen, to listen with the ear of the heart, to pay attention to the pulse, the heartbeat of God within the heart of the world.

Jotting in autumn journal 2011

Breaking open, breaking through and the fresh outpouring of life

There have been situations in recent years when I have felt out of control, no longer able to manage what was going on around and within me, and I have written concerning these circumstances later in the book. Paradoxically, it was within these scary thresholds that I sensed a breaking open, a breaking through and a fresh outpouring of life. This was accompanied by what felt like an unquenchable longing for music, and yet what formally had brought solace, inspiration, joy had lost the sense of resonance; it jarred. There were a few exceptions, like an old tape-recording of great hymns sung on an unforgettable evening in the Civic Hall in Portsmouth, harmonies and words touching my soul and in my convalescence bringing me to tears. I've lost that tape – surely it lies hidden within the pile of everything, somewhere? Chants sung by the Taizé Community also held me through some of the darkest of nights.

I wrote a letter to a friend during the autumn of 2011 while convalescing from surgery. For four months I waited, waited for a long open wound to heal following a bypass operation in my left leg. Medically this is known as a fasciotomy.[1] My intention in beginning to write was to acknowledge the longing within the lost resonances and to start to explore what was emerging within the breaking open, breaking through and the fresh outpouring of life. So here are a few of the jottings from my journal and parts of letters and poems received during that period. My hope is that within my apparent randomness there are some resonances for you.

Where to begin?

I begin with an acknowledgement that what I explore may be difficult to express in words and also that my longing to share the mystery of these things with others has met with a notable silence.

Herons over the loch, echoes

In our childhood my brother and I were taken by our parents to the Isle of Skye, where they had come for their honeymoon. In the evenings I scrambled up into the hills behind the farm and sat there, alone yet not alone, watching the herons swooping over the surface of the loch below, listening to them, also hearing the echoes. As evening turned toward night I gazed upwards into the silence of the starry skies. For the first time, I encountered what now I choose to call an inner yet cosmic music. Perhaps that's all I can say of that for now.

Balloons

While resting last week I heard a considerable noise in the playground next door to our home, and on looking out of the bedroom window saw what I imagined to be everyone in the life of the school (a Roman Catholic Primary) congregating, each person holding a large coloured balloon with a piece of paper attached. Then on the stroke of 11 o'clock there was a communal countdown – 10, 9, 8, 7, 6, 5, 4, 3, 2, 1 – and then a great cloud of balloons rose up accompanied by wondrous cheers transforming into a beautiful song – everyone drawn into a joyous, swaying movement. Oh, how I wish I could sing and move like that.

A few days later I asked our neighbour's children what had been the source of such joy. I discovered that each child had written a message to God asking for help to become what they could become in their lives. 'So what did you write?' I asked.

'I asked God to help me to become the goalkeeper for the England women's football team,' was the reply.

Discovering the tones that resonate, liberate ...

As It Is in Heaven is the English title of a beautiful Swedish film. It tells of a world-famous conductor suffering from chronic illness and exhaustion retiring to Norrland in the far north of Sweden, to the village where he had endured terrible bullying as a child. The young musician is slowly drawn out of his chosen isolation, and with some reluctance agrees to listen to the local choir: only to listen and perhaps offer some advice. Gradually he starts to help the choir, and in time rediscovers his own joy in music. The choir's expectation is that he will bring music with him; draw them into the world of the great choral tradition. Quite the reverse happens: the conductor helps them to discover the tones that already resonate within their hearts and souls, and what can happen when their voices blend into one song. The story is one of transformational human unfolding and interconnectedness. A remarkable, poignant film.[2]

***

John belonged to the church community in Lancaster Road, Notting Hill. His nature was wild yet gentle, his appearance rough, uncared for; his illness was schizophrenia. On occasions during worship John would suddenly burst into shouting and yelling and rush toward the preacher. On other occasions John would ask if he could sing – and when John sang it was with great beauty, a poignancy that arose from the deep places of his soul. Peter, our organist, who knew John well and loved him, waited before quietly picking up the melody on the organ. Such beauty from within such dark complexity.

***

Jo was born with cerebral palsy and was unable to speak or to move any of her limbs. She communicated through a small light pointer attached to a sweatband on her head and beaming onto a qwerty letter board on her lap. During one of our gatherings for those living with disabilities I asked, 'Jo, what about music? What is the significance of music for you?' And immediately she tapped out her reply, 'I long to set to music the poems of Thomas Traherne, George Herbert and John Donne.' Slowly she spelt out her words telling of the music that lay within her and how much she wanted to express it. And our question remained, 'But how?' And she shrugged her shoulders.

***

This morning I just happened to go downstairs around 11 o'clock to make a drink and saw someone standing, looking into our front window; it was Harry. I opened the door and invited him to come in for a drink. Harry had a stroke a few years ago leaving him semi-paralysed on the right-hand side of his body, including his arm; his speech also was severely impaired leaving him able only to stutter 'De, de, de, de …' His mind remains clear though, his passion to communicate intense. It was obvious that Harry wanted to communicate something about his wife, Shirley: how much he loved her, and about Liverpool where she came from. And Harry wept and wept.

Later, as we slowly walked the short stretch from our home to the busy Church Road junction where I planned to see him safely across the road, I thought: What about Harry and singing? So I asked, 'Can you still sing, Harry?' Immediately he smiled and found the melody lines of some of his most well-loved hymns, his heart hymns. We agreed that next time we met we would sing together (and that is what we did).

Meanwhile, on the other side of the busy junction, an African woman carrying a heavy load of shopping saw us, stopped, waited and, while keeping watch on the traffic, helped Harry across the road and up onto the pavement. Clearly they knew each other. 'He is Africa man!' she said more than once. 'He is a wonderful man.' On that we both agreed. Shirley and Harry had both been teachers in Namibia.

Resonances that touch the soul
(jotting in my autumn journal 2011)

Dr Candace Pert is a research professor in the department of physiology and biophysics at Georgetown University Medical Centre in Washington. In her book *Molecules of Emotion* she tells about what it has been like as a woman working in the hierarchical, male medical world: her rejection, humiliation, isolation, hurt pride; her continuing courage, determination and integrity in the search for truth. She has a Jewish background and tells how at one of her lowest points she had been walking by a local Methodist church, nursing the usual grudges. The sound of voices carrying a beautiful melody drew her inside, where she met a choir rehearsing. Spontaneously, she expressed her appreciation of their wonderful music, and they invited her to join in, and she did, as an alto. And she learned to sing the great hymns with their resonances that touch the soul, telling of healing and hope, forgiveness and reconciliation. [3]

Note: Dr Candace Pert died in 2013.

'*My body* lies over the ocean ...'

Kjell is my wife's cousin and lives in their home village in central Sweden. He has lived with Parkinson's disease for over 25 years. At times his hands shake, his head lies to one side, but he has become an artist, a poet, and he sings. When Kjell sings his favourite song people listen: '*Nobody knows the trouble I've seen, Lord, nobody knows but Jesus ...*'

Over the telephone Kjell told me about the visits from the Director of music of their village church; together they sing. Kjell speaks of *'our inner music, our inner songs'*. He asked: 'Donald, which is your soul song, and will you sing it to me?'

A few weeks later on Skype, to Kjell's surprise, and also my own, I sang to Kjell a setting of the 'Agnus Dei', which I first heard sung by the congregation of St Clement's Church in the back streets of Notting Hill: *'O Lamb of God, who takes away the sins of the world.'* Kjell and I have a shared heart song: *'My body* lies over the ocean, *my body* lies over the sea … bring back, bring back, oh, bring back *my body* to me …'

Two letters
(received during the long period of convalescence in autumn 2011)

I recall our friend Israel Selvanayagam being invited to address the Forum for Spiritual Directors in Birmingham on 'Indian Spirituality'. He drew our attention to the significance in Hinduism of the primal resonances within the intoning of 'Om …'

More and more I wonder about this primal Om.

In a letter, Israel wrote:

> *'Sometimes the unfathomable depth creates a vibration that touches our nerves and senses. We do not dictate the particular wavelength of that vibration. But we can expect its movement to be more than walking the second mile, more than a simple embrace and encompassing and much closer than what we think as the closest point within us … When depth calls depth we do not hear, yet the vibration and echo should be somewhere in this mysterious calling.'*

Geoffrey Ainger, a friend from our Notting Hill years, wrote:

> *'As I have no doubt told you (perhaps too many times) one of my favourite cartoons I found many decades ago in* The New

Yorker: *A heavily horn-rimmed psychiatrist is behind his large, imposing desk. Before him, sitting alert on the carpet of the capacious consulting room, is a small dog. "Tell me," says the psychiatrist. "Can anyone else hear the whistle?" ... In the sharing of our experience of adversity, you become aware, from time to time, not of a whistle, but of an echo of a primal music "when all the morning stars sang together" ... Isn't it amazing that the witness to such a fundamental, though hidden harmony should be made by someone in the dark grip of affliction? You belong to that precious company of rumour-mongers whose mixture of stammering, silence and laughter bears witness to the glad strangeness of the gospel. Meanwhile, we totter on.'*

I've missed Job's testimony to *the morning stars singing together and all the heavenly beings shouting for joy when the foundations of the earth were laid* (Jb 38:4–7).

'You didn't know that you were a song'

I once met the Swedish poet Ylva Eggehorn, and asked her about her short poem, 'Stå stilla i smärtan'. She told of the painful complexity within which the poem came into being.

> *Stand still in the pain,*
> *rooted in that in you which is light.*
> *Let the sword go through you.*
> *Maybe it is not*
> *a sword at all.*
> *Maybe it is a tuning fork.*
> *You become a note.*
> *You become the music*
> *you always longed*
> *to hear.*
> *You didn't know that you were*
> *a song.*

Ylva Eggehorn[4]

Resistance, protest, outrage and a transformative inner music

In 1982 the parting gift from the church in Notting Hill enabled me to visit the families and friends of the Caribbean members of our congregation, in Jamaica, Barbados and Trinidad and Tobago. Kerstin's mother had been diagnosed with cancer and naturally Kerstin wanted to be with her. I visited Jamaica on my own, Annika, our daughter, joined me in Barbados, and we shared the rest of the journey together. We were in the Caribbean soon after the American invasion of Grenada. During our time in Barbados I met Allan Kirton, the young General Secretary to the Caribbean Council of Churches. Courageously, he had spoken out prophetically against the invasion, only to be called into the government offices in Bridgetown and told that he be silent. There were churches that banned Allan from preaching.

It was during this period that subversive anti-war songs/calypsos were being written, and subsequently banned from the radio, television and public places.

On one memorable night in Bridgetown, Annika and I attended a concert, and as the final applause faded away the mood changed, and to our surprise the band quietly started up again and everyone, *everyone* in the audience rose to their feet, smiling, swaying; there was no singing, only joyous, defiant dancing. It was 'Boots', the song banned by the government, the forbidden song that protested against the diversion of public money away from poverty programmes and into equipping the army with 'boots'. I can still feel the rhythms, see the swaying bodies, hear the laughing – defiant, liberating.

***

The documentary *5 Broken Cameras* was filmed by Palestinian farmer Emad Burnat in the West Bank village of Bil'in. It tells the story of the villagers' non-violent response to the Israeli military when they arrived on the pretext of protecting building companies

erecting a wall separating the Palestinian village and an Israeli set-
tlement. The villagers approach the line of soldiers singing, beating
their drums, and asking the soldiers why they had come. Why were
they protecting those who had stripped their olive plantations?[5]

***

Ben worked for the Probation Service, and in his earlier years
toured the world with the hard rock band Godflesh. Their music
emerged in the late 1980s, the end of the Thatcher years – harsh
sounds of protest from working-class East Birmingham youth: *'a
barking back'*, *'an act of cleansing and purifying'* from so much that
poisoned the air and dehumanised political and social systems,
holding the people down.

I have written about my encounter with Godflesh later in the book.[6]

Invitations to parties

Some of us don't do parties, don't do singing and don't do dancing.
Perhaps because we are shy; perhaps because we are fragile. Our
heart may sing, our eyes laugh, our feet tap, our body gently sway,
and still within us there can be a primal hesitation in letting go
and following where the music may lead us.

'He heard the music but would not go in.'

There was a huge party to celebrate Gwen Blandford's 80th
birthday. Gwen was a much-loved Methodist minister in Smeth-
wick and Balsall Heath in Birmingham, and had also been a music
teacher: one who had found and released the music within her
pupils. Gwen asked that an act of worship be included and invited
me to preach. Predictably, Gwen provided not only the Gospel
passage upon which to preach but the precise verse for preaching.
It was the story of the prodigal son returning from squandering
his father's inheritance, impoverished, chastened, yet welcomed
by his father who *'seeing him afar off ran to embrace him'*. The
father implored the older brother to lay down his jealous resent-

ments and join the party. *'Now the elder son was in the field; and when he came and approached the house he heard the music and dancing … Then he became angry and refused to go in'* (Luke 15:25–28). This was the verse I was invited to preach on.

***

During Refugee Week many years ago Kerstin went to the cathedral with a Muslim family from Iran; there was to be a party for asylum seekers and refugees. The Dean was a courageous, generous and imaginative man. He made arrangements for all the pews to be cleared to the walls for music and dancing; tables were put up for groups to sit around and eat and drink. There was circle dancing by the Muslims, who drew people in; there was a Jewish choir. People sang and everyone clapped. Kerstin came home declaring that she had *never* been to such a gathering before. It was as if the asylum seekers and refugees were granted a momentary taste of freedom and joy.

'The music of God in every happening' …

It was during this same period in the autumn of 2011 that a friend gave me a book called *Old Age: Journey into Simplicity*, by Helen M. Luke. It was deceptively short and spoke to me in my exploration of an inner music:

> *'Now we may begin to hear that new language which is more in the nature of spontaneous song. The "music of God" in every happening, whether of pain or joy. The music is unique in you and in me and in every detail of the incarnate world, but however simple or complex, however loud or soft, it will harmonise with the great "unstruck sound" of the totality. Dante in the* Paradiso *writes of the sound of the angels in the white rose as the humming of bees. It sounds through the entire universe. When we begin to hear it we approach the Mercy, and may sing with Angelus Silesius, "the rose has not why, it flowers because it flowers".*[7]

Thomas Merton, the Cistercian monk, wrote of *the music playing within us, playing within the created order, the hidden music, underground, a river, deep within the rock of our lives, coursing along in the dark.* [8]

Echoes of a banquet for all people

I love the concluding prayer in the Methodist Eucharistic liturgy:

> 'We thank you, Lord, that you have fed us in this sacrament, united us with Christ and given us a foretaste of the heavenly banquet prepared for all people.' [9]

A banquet for all people, yes, prepared for all people.

'They hear as music what we hear as pain'

Shortly before he died, an old friend, Brian Duckworth, visited our home. As he rose to leave he put his arm around my shoulder and said: 'Thank God for us,' and I responded, almost without thinking: 'And thank God for those who have to live with us too.' He then turned and replied, 'I want to hear these words on my dying day: *They hear as music what we hear as pain.*'

I have wondered what Brian meant.

***

In *The Divine Comedy* Dante sees the glory of the angel standing on the further side of the fire and rejoices in the beauty of his singing: *'Holy Souls, there is no way on or round but through the bite of fire; in, then, and come! Nor be you deaf to what is sung beyond.'* [10]

***

Since beginning this writing I joined a U3A music appreciation group, facilitated by Bob, a retired professor of music. In our first session, and for two whole hours, we were drawn into Beethoven's

Missa Solemnis, its structure and heart. Those monthly sessions became more than I could have longed for.

Bob recently died and I am among those who sorely miss him.

Notes:

1. 'A fasciotomy is a surgical procedure where the fascia is cut to relieve tension or pressure, commonly to treat the resulting loss of circulation to an area of tissue or muscle. It is a limb-saving procedure when used to treat acute compartment syndrome.' (From Wikipedia)

2. *Så Som i Himmelen*, Director: Kay Pollak, Kino Lorber Films, 2004

3. See *Molecules of Emotion: The Science behind Mind-Body Medicine*, by Candace B. Pert, Simon and Schuster, 1999. Used by permission of the Estate of Candace B. Pert

4. 'Stå stilla i smärtan', translated from the Swedish by Kerstin Eadie. Used by permission of Ylva Eggehorn

5. *5 Broken Cameras*, Directors: Emad Burnat, Guy Davidi, Kino Lorber Films, 2011

6. See 'The return of Godflesh: barking back', p.166

7. From *Old Age: Journey into Simplicity*, by Helen M. Luke, Parabola Books, p.93. Used by permission of the Apple Farm Community and the Executor for Helen M. Luke's literary estate

8. Thomas Merton, source unknown

9. From *The Methodist Worship Book*, 'Holy Communion Ordinary Seasons' (1), p.197, Methodist Publishing

10. From *Dark Wood to White Rose: Journey and Transformation in Dante's Divine Comedy*, by Helen M. Luke. Parabola Books, 1995. Used by permission of the Apple Farm Community and the Executor for Helen M. Luke's literary estate

Changing the world, 'Yes' to rejoining the revolution (a work in progress)

'I became a dreamer wanting to change the world and also one who was confronted by the reality of human violence, suffering and death in recent history' ...

This writing began in the chapel of the beautiful St Beuno's Spirituality Centre in North Wales, on the last full day of an eight-day silent retreat.

These days have been thrilling, wonderful in ways I could not have expected, significant in ways I find hard to express. I am hearing within myself: *'So, I have rejoined the revolution!'* Understandably there were smiles and curiosity when I later shared this with others.

I want to be in touch with whatever this might mean.

The silence during the eight days was punctuated by a daily visit from Father Stan. I know little of him save that he is a Colomban priest who has worked in Tanzania and who, having lost the use of both his legs twenty-five years ago, now lives from a wheelchair. In the first session he smiled and asked, 'Who is Donald?'

The telling of my story includes the unfolding of many interwoven stories and within them my 'yes' – a series of them! One strand lies within what I choose to call a 'worldly mysticism', and I am not going to attempt to explain that now. I hope this mystery will emerge within what follows.

My early awakenings include a 'coming alive' as a human being, wonder within creation, deepening awareness and attentiveness of contemporary world affairs and a growing consciousness of our perplexing depths as human beings. My education was at Kingswood in Bath, a Methodist public school, a place of rich resources and privileged opportunities. Among my memories are the conversations with Mr Sackett, the headmaster, a man most of us pupils held in awe. Early in my life at Kingswood, during the annual pupil meeting with Mr Sackett with the purpose of reviewing my school report, he asked, 'Eadie, what's it all about? Life. Who are we, where have we come from, where are we going to? Eadie, go away and think about it.' He gave me books to read in the school holidays, like *My Dear Timothy*, by Victor Gollancz. I became an avid reader absorbed by books that told of those who had set out to explore the world and also to transform it. I became a dreamer wanting to change the world and also one who was con-fronted by the reality of human violence, suffering and death in recent history, and in particular at that time, in Kenya, where the Mau Mau were resisting white European farmers.

This was a period when I became fascinated by Jesus, the man of Galilee, his disturbing teaching, his shocking inclusiveness, his way of loving and forgiving, his suffering and dying. I recoiled from some preaching about the Passion and was mystified by some expositions of the doctrines of the Cross. I grew in amaze-ment as to how, from somewhere deep within him, Jesus found the resources to seek the good of those who were threatened by him and plotted to both remove and destroy him, *'Father, forgive them, they do not know what they are doing.'* This way of living, this kind of loving was beyond my comprehension and I wanted not only to learn more but also to give the rest of my life in attempting 'to have a go' at living his way. I gave my 'yes' to wanting to be a follower of the Way of Jesus.

I have an old, loved and battered folder which for many, many years has held my sermons, talks, lectures, addresses. On the front is a small faded picture stuck on with Sellotape: a photograph of a pair of feet walking on stony ground. Whose feet? I don't know but probably they belong to a poor Indian farm labourer out in the fields, perhaps sowing seed on stony ground. Why this image? It's about the 'yes' to walking the talk, about the intention to speak in such a way that inspires and encourages those who listen also to walk the talk, day by day. This is where the revolution is lived.

Within these depths the new identity, the new humanity is formed.

During the eight days of silence at St Beuno's I read through the whole of Mark's Gospel with the intention of learning more of the way of friendship lived by Jesus, his embrace of the untouchable, his shocking inclusiveness. There are keys texts which enunciate the foolishness, the contrariness, the provocation, the subversion, the threat, the revolutionary manifesto encountered through those who live the Way of Jesus. They are summarised in this passage written by Paul:

> *Let love be genuine; hate what is evil, hold fast to what is good; love one another with mutual affection; outdo one another in showing honour. Do not lag in zeal, be ardent in spirit, serve the Lord. Rejoice in hope, be patient in suffering, persevere in prayer. Contribute to the needs of the saints; extend hospitality to strangers.*

> *Bless those who persecute you; bless and do not curse them. Rejoice with those who rejoice, weep with those who weep. Live in harmony with one another; do not be haughty, but associate with the lowly; do not claim to be wiser than you are. Do not repay anyone evil for evil, but take thought for what is noble in the sight of all. If it is possible, so far as it depends on you, live peaceably with all. Beloved, never avenge yourselves, but leave room for the wrath of God; for it is written, 'Vengeance is mine, I will repay, says the Lord.' No, 'if your enemies are hungry, feed them; if they are thirsty, give them something to drink; for by doing this you will heap burning coals on their heads.' Do not be overcome by evil, but overcome evil with good.*

> Romans 12:9–21 (NRSV)[1]

The desire to change the world and to wrestle with the paradoxes within our human nature became the terrain where the first fires were lit. The only way I could imagine holding all this was within one vocation, namely to become a Methodist minister.

These growing passions I shared with Mr Sackett; and his response was 'Eadie, go down a coalmine, go where men sweat and swear, learn what life is about and if you still want to be a minister, God bless you.'

He earthed me, grounded me. I followed his guidance and on leaving the comforts and privileges of Kingswood went to work, not in a coalmine, but in Lister's Mill, a large wool and textile factory in my home city of Bradford. My work was in a warehouse with all sorts and conditions of humanity, including Slavic refugees and people released from Armley Prison in Leeds. The experience was more than I could have imagined and soon my world view, my identity, assumptions and values were threatened, challenged and I wanted to quit. My father stood in my tracks, confronted me, and persuaded me to 'stay with it and see it through'. Slowly I became politicised and learned why joining a trade union was important. I made friends with my work mates, especially with Doug, the youngest person on the basement shop floor; with Peter who, it was said, had been a bodyguard to the Tsar of Russia and who had become a praying Bible-reading Christian; with Endil from Estonia, a quiet and good man, who later invited me to join his family for an evening meal in their home; and with Rick, who had been in prison. When I left the factory to go to theological college it was Rick who addressed me, 'So you are leaving us and going to study to be a minister and never again will you share life as you have done with us. And I am sad.' I wept the day I left the factory.

The years in the warehouse reshaped my world view and also the core of my vocation. I have never wanted to be a churchy minister. My commitment has been to the world and to the lives of ordinary people.

In the summer of 1960 I was fortunate to be a delegate to the European Ecumenical Youth Assembly in Lausanne, Switzerland, prior to the meeting of the World Council of Churches in New Delhi. Eighteen hundred young people from thirty countries attended the Assembly. It was an inspiration. Kerstin was a delegate from Sweden and we shared the life and work of the same core study group, but that is another story. Kerstin says that she was attracted to this *'young Englishman so fired with social passion'*.

Lausanne was for some a gateway into the student uprisings in Europe in the 1960s, the struggle for justice and peace through the anti-apartheid movement, the Campaign for Nuclear Disarmament, the campaign for the homeless through Shelter, and the long work of reconciliation between Catholic and Protestant through the founding of the Corrymeela Community in Northern Ireland.

I was inspired by the lives and writings of Mahatma Gandhi in India, Martin Luther King in the southern USA, Daniel Berrigan, the radical anti-war priest in the US, Toyohiko Kagawa in the slums of Tokyo, and Thomas Merton, the Cistercian monk in Gethsemani in Kentucky. Texts from these writers have become foundational for me, and I continue to return to them.

The Croi

So where did the statement *'I'm rejoining the revolution'* come from?

The days of silence at St Beuno's gave me time to recall our visit to the Corrymeela Community in March of that year. The Community was founded 50 years ago and has been committed to the long work of reconciliation in Northern Ireland. Inderjit Bhogal has been a good friend for many years and was the leader of the Corrymeela Community at the time of our visit.

On arrival, Inderjit took us to 'the Croi', Irish for core: two beautifully designed rooms carved deep into rock, shaped like a heart. I lay on the carpeted floor while a handful of others sat on cushions. On a small low central table Inderjit placed a candle alongside a cross and an open Bible. He spoke of the Croi as womb, the place of gestation, of waiting, of nurture, and of the Croi as tomb. The candle was lit and we entered silence for half an hour. I remained primarily within the image of the heart, while becoming aware of the beating of the pulse. After a prayer of blessing Inderjit spoke of the origins and history of Corrymeela, and also about what it means to sustain the long work of reconciliation. He led us into an adjacent room, also very beautiful, with chairs set in a circle: a room set aside for listening to those whose experiences within 'the Troubles' were so painfully different.

Our sharing in the silence of the Croi became for me a mystical experience: the sense of heart and pulse among torn communities that have known such violence, so much inhuman suffering and within which some continue to reach out toward understanding 'the other' with compassion.

Later we heard stories from those whose prayer for reconciliation was lived: they 'walked the talk', and sometimes at great cost. They had become revolutionaries daring to live a new way, daring to break the patterns of prejudice, fear and hatred, daring to be counter-cultural, daring to build bridges between alienated people and communities in Northern Ireland.

I am not sure what I am saying when I speak of the desire to rein-habit the core, the centre, the essence which is the heart of the revolution. What emerges as the heart lies within the calling of Jesus: 'Love with my love.'

What also emerged from those days of silence at St Beuno's was the renewed awareness of the significance of friendship. I have been given the gift of both receiving and offering friendship. This has become one of my paths of following. I return to the writing of Henri Nouwen and his description of the nature of friendship:

> *'When we honestly ask ourselves which persons in our lives mean the most to us, we often find that it is those who, instead of giving much advice, solutions, or cures, have chosen rather to share our pain and touch our wounds with a gentle and tender hand. The friend who can be silent with us in a moment*

of despair or confusion, who can stay with us in an hour of grief or bereavement, who can tolerate not-knowing, not-curing, not-healing and face with us the reality of our power-lessness, that is the friend who cares.'[2]

Have you changed the world?

I live increasingly with a sense of my own mortality, of endings, yet the eight days of silence at St Beuno's opened up so much yet to be explored, drawing me into what feels wonderful, thrilling and also scary.

During the last session with Father Stan he asked, 'So you have changed the world, Donald?' I spontaneously laughed. 'No,' I replied, confused and embarrassed. 'You *have* changed the world, Donald,' he said firmly. I'm beginning to comprehend what this might now mean.

This is why I continue to press on with preparing this book.

Texts from some of those writers who have become foundational for me and to which I continue to return:

Thomas Merton was a Cistercian monk who discovered in the solitude of his hermitage both his own humanity and also an inter-connectedness with people all around the world.

> *'He who attempts to act and to do things for others or for the world without deepening his own self-understanding, freedom, integrity and capacity to love, will not have anything to give others. He will communicate to them nothing but the contagion of his own obsessions, his aggressiveness, his ego-centred ambitions, his delusions about ends and means, his doctrinaire prejudices and ideas.'*[3]

> *'Merton's deep conviction [was] that contemplation is basically a social matter, and that silence, solitude, prayer, are not private properties, but belong to the people with and for whom he lives.*

*His conviction that solitude didn't belong to him as a possession
came forth out of his heart-rending discovery that Auschwitz,
Hiroshima, Vietnam and Watts were present in the intimate core
of his own being. There where he thought he could be alone with
himself, he found that he wasn't one man, but that in him lived
mankind, in all its misery but also in its longing for love.'*[4]

Martin Luther King was President of the Southern Christian Leadership Conference and co-pastor of the Ebenezer Baptist Church,
in Atlanta, Georgia. He led the dramatic 'walk for freedom' in
Montgomery, Alabama, which resulted in bus desegregation, and
was active in the Albany Movement. He was assassinated on April
4, 1968 in Memphis, Tennessee.

*'For more than three centuries American Negroes have been
battered by the iron rod of oppression, frustrated by day and
bewildered by night by unbearable injustice, and burdened with
the ugly weight of discrimination. Forced to live with these
shameful conditions, we are tempted to become bitter and to
retaliate with a corresponding hate. But if this happens, the new
order we seek will be little more than a duplicate of the old
order. We must in strength and humility meet hate with love …*

*To our most bitter opponents we say: "We shall match your
capacity to inflict suffering by our capacity to endure suffering.
We shall meet your physical force with soul force. Do to us what
you will, and we shall continue to love you. We cannot in all good
conscience obey your unjust laws, because non-cooperation with
evil is as much a moral obligation as is cooperation with good.
Throw us in jail, and we shall still love you. Send your hooded
perpetrators of violence into our community at the midnight hour
and beat us and leave us half dead, and we shall still love you.
But be ye assured that we will wear you down by our capacity to
suffer. One day we shall win freedom, but not only for ourselves.
We shall so appeal to your heart and conscience that we shall
win you in the process, and our victory will be a double victory."*

Love is the most durable power in the world. This creative force, so beautifully exemplified in the life of our Christ, is the most potent instrument available in mankind's quest for peace and security.' [5]

'One of the great liabilities of history is that all too many people fail to remain awake through great periods of social change. Every society has its protectors of the status quo and its fraternities of the indifferent who are notorious for sleeping through revolutions. But today, our very survival depends on our ability to stay awake, to adjust to new ideas, to remain vigilant and to face the challenge of change. The large house in which we live demands that we transform this world-wide neighbourhood into a world-wide brotherhood. Together we must learn to live as brothers or together we will be forced to perish as fools.' [6]

Notes:

1. Passage from NRSV copyright 1989, Division of Christian Education of the National Council of the Churches of Christ in the United States of America. Used by permission. All rights reserved.

2. Excerpted from *Out of Solitude: Three Meditations on the Christian Life*, by Henri J. M. Nouwen. Copyright ©1974, 2004 by Ave Maria Press®, Inc., P.O. Box 428, Notre Dame, IN 46556, www.avemariapress.com. Used with permission of the publisher.

3. From *Thomas Merton: Spiritual Master: Essential Writings*, Lawrence Cunningham (Ed), Paulist Press, 1992, p.375. Used by permission of Paulist Press.

4. Excerpt from *Thomas Merton Contemplative Critic*, by Henri Nouwen ©1968 Henri Nouwen, is reprinted with the permission of the Henri Nouwen Legacy Trust.

5. Copyright © 1963 Dr. Martin Luther King, Jr. © renewed 1991 Coretta Scott King.

6. Copyright © 1967 Dr. Martin Luther King, Jr. © renewed 1995 Coretta Scott King. 5 & 6 Reprinted by arrangement with The Heirs to the Estate of Martin Luther King Jr., c/o Writers House as agent for the proprietor New York, NY.

On being human

The passion has been to transform the world and also to deepen awareness of what it means to be human.

My own journey into a more reflective awareness of our complex humanity came through a long period in Jungian psychoanalysis during the 1970s while living and working in Notting Hill. My work included paying attention to my identity as an adopted person and what that means for my being human. I have written about this search for identity later in the book.[1] I recall in our first session Bani Shorter, my analyst, saying, 'Donald, there are three in this room, not two. There is One present with us who can take us to places we could not otherwise go.' Bani was baptised and received into the Russian Orthodox Church during the time we worked together.

Increasingly I recognise our 'primary call' to be that of being real, real rather than religious: to enter the depths of our humanity and within everything to be open, open to the companionship of the silent, hidden yet truth-revealing compassionate One.

Our second vocation is to be a follower of Jesus Christ; to be human in the way Jesus was, this enables us to fulfil our first vocation. Rowan Williams, in his writing about 'holiness', says *'the way that Jesus talks about holiness at the Last Supper is so transforming. Holiness there is seen as going into the heart of where it's most difficult for human beings to be human. Jesus goes "outside the city"; he goes to the place where people suffer and are humiliated, the place where people throw stuff out, including other people.'*[2]

Our journey into becoming human concerns our relationships; we encounter the 'otherness' of the 'other' in our being open to one another, including the stranger in the midst. No one expresses this more poignantly than Archbishop Desmond Tutu when he speaks of '*ubuntu*'.

'*[Ubuntu] speaks of the very essence of being human ... We say, "A person is a person through other persons" ... A person with ubuntu is open and available to others, affirming of others, does not feel threatened that others are able and good, for he or she has a proper self-assurance that comes from knowing that he or she belongs in a greater whole and is diminished when others are humiliated or diminished, when others are tortured or oppressed, or treated as if they were less than who they are.*'[3]

The human condition

In 2008 I was asked to write on 'the human condition' and chose to explore our essential interrelatedness in living into the transformative way.[4] I began with a description of what has proved to be a transformative encounter:

The invitation was to remove racist slogans daubed on the walls of a railway bridge. Members of the local Liberal Party and Communist Party planned a protest for midday on a Sunday morning, the time when the people of the Churches would be moving from worship into the fellowship of coffee and biscuits. Could we, would we change the time of services in order to take our place in that neighbourhood ritual? We did; and the conversations that Sunday lunchtime led not only to a public Christian/Marxist debate but also to deep and rigorous discussion in each other's homes. We talked about the ideological base from which each developed their world view, the political realities and ethical issues to be wrestled with, also the nature of the human condition.

We belonged to that generation in the 1960s who lived and worked with social hope, passionately campaigned for the removal of apartheid in South Africa, for nuclear disarmament through CND and for the homeless in Britain through Shelter. With Martin Luther King we dreamed dreams and also confronted human wickedness.

So, what of the human condition?

Our first vocation is to be a human being; to be fully human, it is for this that we are born. It is to be real rather than religious, honest rather than heroic. The journey into our humanity includes befriending our many selves, our many inner voices, becoming aware of our capacity for love and hate: for human kindness and for cruelty, for truth-telling and for deceit and manipulation, for being creative and for being destructive.

The relationship between our own inner and outer worlds is complex. We use noise and busyness to protect ourselves from listening, fearing what awaits us in the silence and solitude of those depths. Our tendency is to project elsewhere the dark within us, the bits that we don't like and find hard to accept. Only slowly and painfully do we embrace this perplexing, interacting mixture of good and evil, light and shadow, creation and destruction as belonging to the wonder and terror of who we are. The wounds from the past may fester, disfigure and imprison but they may also be enfolded into our greater wholeness, our deeper humanity.

A friend wrote of his discovery of '*a freedom within the prison of illness, handicap or cell*'.[5] To be human is to live this freedom within limitation, frailty and complexity. It is to dare to come out of hiding from behind our masks, to be open and honest, to be gentle, to let tears of laughter and joy stain our face, to own our rage, to be passionate, to make mistakes, to recover our playfulness. It is also to embrace pain, to become pain-bearers, absorbing in our bodies evil, suffering, grief and shame willingly.

To be human also includes the acknowledgement of our interconnectedness with terrible atrocities.

In all these things we may discern the marks of a profound humanity within which some see the humanity of Jesus. What has to happen, I wonder, for our churches to become truly human communities, safe places into which we can bring the depths of our humanity?

Many of us are both attracted and scared by the humanity of Jesus; we too easily lose him in religious language, in theological formulae and in certain ways of studying the Bible.

Our testimony is not only that God was in Christ but also that God is in the depths of our own humanity.

To be human is to be drawn into the heart of life, into the heart of God. It is to journey into the deep love of God, the compassion of God.

A poem on being human

Tomas Tranströmer was born in Stockholm in 1931, and died on 26 March, 2015. In 1990, he suffered a stroke which deprived him of his speech and inhibited movement on his right side. In 2011 he won the Nobel Prize for Literature. Following is one of his powerful poems:

> *Inside the huge romanesque church the tourists jostled*
>   *in the half darkness.*
> *Vault gaped behind vault, no complete view.*
> *A few candle-flames flickered.*
> *An angel with no face embraced me*
> *and whispered through my whole body:*
> *'Don't be ashamed of being human, be proud!*
> *Inside you vault opens behind vault endlessly.*
> *You will never be complete, that's how it's meant to be.'*
> *Blind with tears*
> *I was pushed out on the sun-seething piazza*
> *together with Mr and Mrs Jones, Mr Tanaka,*
>   *and Signora Sabatini,*
> *and inside them all vault opened behind vault endlessly.* [6]

Notes:

1. See 'A search for identity, living with adoption', p.69

2. From *Being Disciples: Essentials of the Christian Life*, Rowan Williams, SPCK, 2016. Used by permission of SPCK.

3. Excerpt from *No Future Without Forgiveness* by Desmond Tutu, copyright © 1999 by Desmond Tutu. Used by permission of Doubleday, an imprint of the Knopf Doubleday Publishing Group, a division of Penguin Random House LLC. All rights reserved. From *No Future Without Forgiveness* by Desmond Tutu published by Rider. Reproduced by permission of The Random House Group Ltd. © 1999

4. 'The human condition' was published in *Magnet*, the Methodist magazine, winter, 2008

5. Michael Wilson, a priest and doctor

6. 'Romanesque Arches', by Tomas Tranströmer, from *New Collected Poems*, translated from the Swedish by Robin Fulton, Bloodaxe Books, 2011. Used by permission of Bloodaxe Books

Vulnerability as the heart of transformation

This piece of writing is my way of saying thank you to those 'new companions' I never knew existed and who, while being further on the way than I am, have also been alongside encouraging, challenging, sharing their life wisdom, body wisdom and sometimes their severely tested faith wisdom. We have laughed and cried together: this writing is our song. I am learning the nature of transformation through their vulnerability. My companion during the eight days of silent retreat at St Beuno's urged that I share more widely the story within these stories.

My journal jottings became an address permitting a silent voice to be heard; it became 'a hearing' [1]

I hope those who find biblical images and theological language difficult will nevertheless persist and find enough that resonates here.

I come within the last furlong of my life to offer testimony, a testimony arising from a pilgrimage lived within a terrain in human experience I would never have chosen, a testimony not to God's special protection but rather to God's providential grace.

After his stroke Harry Morton – a man of profound humanity and prophetic passion, a tenacious and compassionate man, widely travelled, deeply respected and greatly loved, a former President of the Methodist Conference and Secretary of the British Council of Churches – lived with his wife, Pat, in a small house in Bow, East London. It is said that only the brave visited him, stayed with him in his broken and sometimes tearful attempts to communicate. On one occasion in his local church when it was a service of Holy Communion, his minister, David Moore, pushed Harry's wheelchair to the front and placed the plate with broken bread on his knees. Harry was unable to lift his arm enough to put bread into the open hands of those who came. So people picked up the bread and perhaps his lips moved enough to murmur, 'The body of Christ.'

I choose to speak on the theme of 'Vulnerability as the heart of transformation'. These are not my words but those of our former Anglican Archbishop Rowan Williams. I want to use these words to reflect on our experience.

I bring a testimony to the 'paschal mystery', the calling to be drawn into the life, suffering, dying and rising of Jesus.

I bring a subversive testimony, the witness of those learning to accept their vulnerability, learning to live with their pain and allowing it to change them, to make them more human, learning to acknowledge liminality, the in-between times, as the context of transformation.

I bring a shocking testimony to a bodily communion linking us, drawing us into solidarity with the suffering, the crucified and the rising body of Christ within all humanity.

And all this in the context of a question: 'What could our experience of the human body, and in particular the experience of those of us who live with impairments, physical and psychological, bring to our being reshaped within the body of Christ?'

The journey from the centre to the edge

I begin by speaking personally and of the journey from the centre to the edge. For much of my life I have taken my body for granted, enjoyed sport, loved walking in the mountains, and through most of my life, and to my shame, worked all hours. In 1987 I commenced my work as Chairman of the Birmingham District of the Methodist Church. Five years later my experience of living with my body changed. I was told that I have a developing degenerative disc disease. There have been three major spinal operations, including the implanting of scaffolding to support the spine. I live with continuing pain and physical limitation. I am unable to stand or sit within pain for more than a few minutes.

I asked those in authority in the Methodist Church for help to minister from a chair, a ministry of stability and availability, and was told that to be a minister I must be mobile and be able to work a three-shift day. I was confused, I was angry and I wept. In later years I have grown to understand this bewildering transition differently.

The journey away from the centre of the busy life of the church to the edge was, paradoxically, a journey deeper into the heart of things. It was unexpected, unwanted and yet became a frightening liberation.

What were the fears? The letting go of identity, role and relationships; living with the new aloneness, the new silence, the new limitation; living with feelings of marginalisation and abandonment; living with the death of the old life, and not being able to imagine a new life with meaning and purpose.

During this time a Jesuit priest, Gerard Hughes, came to visit me and we began to explore what was happening and to interpret the meaning. He accompanied me in this way for nearly 10 years. He helped me both to build a bridge into the future and later to let go dreams and wishes, and to face the emptiness and the waiting within weakness.

Waiting with openness for what is new is not easy. In this experience we become pilgrims. It was Gerry who spoke of the journey from the centre into the borderlands. 'The borderlands,' he said, 'are the place of exploration and discovery; they are the new centre.'

'There will be new companions,' a wise old friend promised. And to my great surprise and joy this has been true. I have met wonderful people I never knew existed. I have encountered prophetic communities.

Much of my time was, and still is, lived in a loved room. And people began to come to the room, not for counselling or therapy but as those who are also pilgrims within the borderlands. Some

seek the life-giving presence of God within this wondrous and terrifying world, and within the story of our lives, others seek help
to live their faithfulness to God within complex and ambiguous
situations. Some are bruised and oppressed through different
forms of religious bullying yet continue to live with a poignant
sense of the 'otherness' and the intimacy of God, and ask if this is
enough. Others appear to be beyond the reach of the church yet
have spiritual needs and ask faith questions. 'This room has
become my church,' one person said. And months later: 'No, *the
world* has become my church.'

Physical limitation, perhaps even divine calling, brings some of
us to a marginalised place. It becomes a conversion experience. A
Director of mission from Rotterdam was one who visited my
room. He spoke of our listening to the voices of people and communities on the margins of society as the mission priority. 'The
borderlands,' he said, 'are the context where God's Spirit works to
convert the Church.'

I have spoken first of the journey from the centre to the edge.

*And second, I speak of the connection between our experience
of our body and the suffering body of Christ.*

We are understandably hesitant to make these connections. For
Paul the imagery of the body was central to both his experience
and his teaching: '*We are all brought into the one body by baptism.*'
(1 Corinthians 12:13). '*When we break bread, is it not a means of
sharing in the body of Christ?*' (1 Cor 10:17). God's call, says Paul,
is for us to be drawn into the mystery of the body of Christ, to
share in his life, suffering, death and resurrection. '*We carry in the
body the death of Jesus, so that the life of Jesus may also be made visible in our body*' (2 Cor 4:10).

The power of the resurrection is only experienced through suffering and the cross. This perplexing paradox belongs to the way
of God in the world.

'*The continuing Passion of God in the world,*' a South African friend said, '*is carried not in abstract ideas but in our human bodies and souls, in our willingness to absorb evil, suffering, grief and shame willingly.*'

I want to introduce you to some of those new companions who have helped me to make these connections.

In 1997 a group of priests, ministers and women in religious orders, all living with physical or psychological impairments, began to meet together in Birmingham. We still come together 4 or 5 times a year, like children to nursery, each of us clutching our sandwiches.

Among them was Angela, an Australian Franciscan nun who lives with MS and is in a wheelchair. Bob, an Anglican priest, who also has MS and is in a wheelchair. Michael, an Anglican priest who lives with depression. Bernie, a La Retraite sister living with a severe spinal condition and pain. John, an Anglican parish priest and his wife, Jo, who was born with cerebral palsy and is in a wheelchair and communicates through a light pointer which beams onto a qwerty keyboard. Geoffrey, also an Anglican priest, who is in the foothills of dementia, and his wife, Janet. Through the years some have died and others have moved away (they are the absent present ones), and others have joined us, including Tony and Ian, both Methodist ministers.

In this group we explore the mystery and meaning of our own suffering: we are real and not heroic; we listen with acceptance and without judgement and learn from the discoveries and insights of others; and we seek the resources to live honestly and compassionately within places of darkness, weariness, frustration, pain and vulnerability. It is our experience that the Church speaks much of pain and suffering but is embarrassed by it.

What are we learning?

We are learning from the experience of dependency; for some this means dependency on others for the toilet, for the washing not only of feet but of the whole body, for receiving food and drink, for being dressed and undressed. We know something of being stripped of roles, responsibilities and masks, of nakedness and exposure, of the loss of dignity, and of humiliation.

Jesus at the end of his life was also stripped, stretched horizontal on a cross, and handed over to others, and in his final hours is shown as almost naked. We are beginning to make the connections between his physical vulnerability and our own experience of weakness. And more, we are discovering theological and spiritual meaning within this experience of our bodies.

We are learning from our experience of pain, of physical and psychological pain interconnected within the memory of the body. We are critical of a Western medical culture that sees pain as simply something to be got rid of, anaesthetised, zapped. We are learning that pain can be a message. We consider the place of pain in the Christian pilgrimage. We are drawn into a contemplation of the Passion of Jesus, what his body bore within that journey, the receiving of the help offered by Simon of Cyrene, the offer and refusal of the drugged wine, the women watching, the soldiers and others drinking and jeering. We live with the mystery that there are those in the world who are the 'pain-bearers', and that sometimes some good comes out of all that suffering, and this has its place in the redemptive process. We use the feeling of solidarity with others in pain as a focus for prayer: victims of earthquakes, floods, hurricanes, tsunamis, HIV/AIDS, TB ... Sometimes we catch glimpses of God in pain.

We are learning from our experience of depression. One person speaks of living in 'a kind of chemicalised numbness', within which he is learning the presence and goodness of God within the sense of the absence of God.

We are learning that theology must not be left to those who are fit and strong. Theology must also be wrestled for through pain and disability; these are the raw materials of our encounters with a mysterious, silent, hidden and powerless God.

We are also learning from something utterly central to our meetings: we laugh and laugh; we leave the meetings energised and with a deeper hope and trust. This is the group above all where we are able to be ourselves, and show others who we really are.

> *I have spoken secondly of our experience of our body and the connection with the body of Christ.*

> *I turn now to speak of the receiving of threatening, 'dangerous gifts' that could transform us.*

It is our experience that the Church finds it difficult to receive the gifts of God through those who live with impairments. We are 'an uncomfortable presence'. In the story of Jesus washing the feet of his disciples, and Simon Peter's difficulty in accepting this, Jesus says *'if you are not able to receive, you can no longer be a disciple of mine'* (John 13:8). Openness to receiving the gifts of God through encounters which may threaten us brings the possibility of transformation, as Simon Peter discovered in his encounter with the Gentile Cornelius (Acts 10:1–48) and as Jesus discovered with the Samaritan woman at the well (John 4:1–15).

I want to introduce more of those 'new companions', and this time in the context of Sarum Theological College, near Salisbury Cathedral. We have had three conferences there, in different ways exploring the faith journey of the impaired pilgrim. On each occasion there were between 20 and 30 people. Among them: Susi, a wheelchair user and a former nurse who worked briefly on the Afghan border of Pakistan; Gordon, a wheelchair user living with MS, who was a Research Fellow in the Physics department of

Birmingham University, and is dependent on the care of his wife, Dot; Ann, who is on the autism spectrum and was the Autism Consultant for the Diocese of Oxford; Sally, another wheelchair user with MS, formerly a teacher of religious education (it is Sally who testifies to 'having fire in her belly and jelly in her knees'), with her husband and carer, Gerald; Ros, a wheelchair user, and a Roman Catholic who has been a Methodist mission partner in Nigeria, a pioneer in mental health provision and a spiritual director; and Peter, who has lived with a spinal condition and chronic pain for too many years, and who had to retire early as a minister. His thesis on the 'Spirituality that emerges from impairment' speaks of 'dangerous gifts', threatening gifts, challenging the traditional view of God and also of God's world. I wish that his thesis could be published and read more widely.

What are the gifts of those living with impairments? We bring our experience of darkness as the context of hidden growing and transformation; we bring our calling to go into the fearful places without being imprisoned by fear; we bring our experience of fragility, of physical weakness, of what it means to trust, and of the mystery of strengthening within our continuing reality; we bring our experience of restoration through touch, embrace and holding, and of an inner healing which is deeper than physical healing; we bring our experience of our bodies, a source of wonder, pleasure and pain, the dwelling place of God, where we meet God in the here and now of our actual humanity; we bring our experience of waiting, waiting into the unknown; we bring our experience of anger, of rage; we bring faith journeys which sometimes include the experience of dereliction, of God-forsakenness, of being apparently without faith in order to grow in faith; we bring our experience of playfulness, of humour, of laughter; we bring our discovery of bread on the edge and of wells of water under our feet, in desert and in destitution, as did both Elijah (1 Kings 17:1–7) and the slave girl Hagar before us (Genesis 21:8–20). I wonder what a Hagar Eucharist would look like; where it is now celebrated and by whom. Consecrated food from heaven is not confined to lie under white cloths in our churches. I bring a testimony not to God's special protection but rather to God's providential grace.

> *I speak of our receiving threatening, 'dangerous gifts' which could transform; gifts from those who are no longer victims but liberators.*

In conclusion

There is one further gift of the Sarum community: a Eucharistic liturgy crafted by Peter Cole in collaboration with Mary Grey, a Roman Catholic professor of theology who was on the leadership team for the first conference, entitled 'The faith journey of impaired pilgrims'. Within the prayer of thanksgiving there is an epiclesis which affirms the continuing presence of God's transforming Spirit, brooding within *'these bodily things'* (for liturgy see p.176).

God's Spirit forms community and transforms through the embodying, the bearing of the marks of the crucified, rising, liberating One, transforms through those in whom grace becomes reality, those who live a messy Magnificat, the blessedness of the children of the Beatitudes.

The Sarum Eucharist also draws us into a shocking solidarity with the crucified and rising body of Christ in all humanity. Through the bread-breaking prayer, by Inderjit Bhogal, we are brought into communion with the countless millions within the human family, the community of the world's pain-bearers, who live with relentless poverty and disease, with environmental poisoning, with hurricane and tsunami, with the traumas of war:

> *'May the broken peoples of the world be blessed.*
> *May we, in our wholeness and brokenness,*
> *be blessed and so become signs of resurrection.'*

Our 'Amen' to the bread, our 'Amen' to the wine, becomes our 'Yes', our yielding into the way of transformation, our being drawn into the embodied pulse, the heartbeat of God within all humanity. *'All for transformation,'* we pray, *'through grace and love made known in Jesus Christ our Lord'*; to which we pray *'Amen.'*

Two quotes to finish:

> *The world has a right to say to the Church: 'Unless I see the marks of the nails in your hands – I will not believe.'*
>
> Stanley Magoba, a former presiding Bishop of the Methodist Church in Southern Africa, speaking to the British Methodist Conference
>
> *May the wounds we carry become signs of resurrection.*
>
> Bishop John Austin

Note:

1. This address has been offered at the following conferences:

    Vinter Konferens, Stockholm, January 2011: an ecumenical conference for representatives of Metodistkyrkan in Sweden, Svenska Baptistsamfundet, Svenska Missionsförbundet. The theme of the conference was 'En Kyrka utan Väggar' ('A Church without Walls').

    The Inclusive Church Conference: Prophets and Seers, St Martin in the Fields, 15-16th October, 2016. The address was recorded on camera because I was not in a condition, physically or emotionally, to negotiate the journey into central London nor sustain the days.

    The Presbyteral Session of the Methodist Conference, 2nd June, 2017.

On the nature of being

In a seminar at the Queen's Foundation in Birmingham I explored the testimony to the presence of God's transforming Spirit within the heart of everything – within creation; within the glory and tragedy of the world we inhabit; within the 'being-ness' of things; within each and every human being, whoever we are, whatever we believe or don't believe, whatever we have done for good or ill.

My companion in the seminar was friend and colleague Renate Wilkinson, a German Lutheran pastor, formerly a chaplain in a large general hospital and also a hospice. Renate has been greatly influenced by the life and death of Dietrich Bonhoeffer. Together we explored seeing through to the heart of things; what some choose to call 'discernment'.

This exploration is my attempt to find words for these mysteries.

We were living in our family's simple, wooden cottage by a lake in the forests of central Sweden. Kerstin's family has lived in that area since the 16th century. We were asked by friends from England, 'But what do you do there?' And the mischievous part of me replied, 'We be.'

Of course there are lots of things to be done: water to be fetched from the well, wood to be chopped for the fire, mats to be scrubbed clean in the lake, clothes to be washed and food to be cooked. But it is also a place for being, a place for gazing, for pondering.

It is a place for wondering about the 'being-ness' of things: the birch-ness of the birch, the blueberry-ness of the blueberry, the orchid-ness of the orchid, the squirrel-ness of the squirrel, the elk-ness of the elk, and the swooping swallow-ness of the swallow. For wondering about the encounter with the being of God within the being of creation. And the being-ness of God within the being-ness of human beings: the Doris-ness of Doris and the Fred-ness of Fred.

In a world with so much that is waiting to be transformed, we may wonder about the significance and the power of 'being'. There is a description of God in the writing of Paul Tillich and made popular by Bishop John Robinson: God as *'the ground of being'*. It has to do with the discovery of immanence within transcendence and of transcendence within immanence. *'The beyond in the midst.'* [1]

Our testimony is to the mystery of God's transforming presence in all things, in all circumstances and in all people. God is in all things even when it does not look like it or feel like it. During a diocesan workshop following the collapse of the Twin Towers in New York on September 11th, 2001, Gerard Hughes said, *'There is no depth of evil where God is not. This is our hope.'* Still I tremble at what this might mean. Also he prayed, *'Spirit of God, hover over the chaos as you did the first chaos and bring from it life and hope.'*

Bishop John Robinson, in his final sermon entitled 'Living with cancer' preached in Trinity College, Cambridge, said, *'Two years ago I found myself having to speak at the funeral of a sixteen-year-old girl who had died in our Yorkshire dale. I said stumblingly that God was to be found in the cancer as much as the sunset. That I firmly believed, but it was an intellectual statement. Now I have had to ask if I can say it of myself, which is a much greater test.'* [2]

Alan Lewis, a professor of theology and also a cancer patient, testifies in his remarkable book *Between Cross and Resurrection: A Theology of Holy Saturday* to *'divine fertility'* within the context of the grave, the tomb and the descent into hell. [3]

There is a big difference between saying God causes suffering, wills it, and saying God is in it and will redeem it.

We are right to shudder and also to wonder when we enter the Eucharistic affirmation: *'Heaven and earth are full of your glory.'* There is an old Jewish prayer: *'Blessed art Thou, Holy One of blessings, whose presence fills all creation'*, and an old hymn with the line: *'in all life Thou livest, the true life of all'*. [4]

Some of us need reminding that prayer is more than something we do when we curl up in some religious corner. Prayer belongs to the nature of God. God's Spirit prays within us, prays within all our faculties, and not just those with religious labels attached.

The letter to the Romans (8:22) testifies to God's Spirit groaning within the whole created universe as in the pangs of birth: a groaning within the travails of Palestinian and Israeli communities, within the long chill winter in Afghanistan, within the cruel shudders of earth tremors, within the forgotten earthquake communities of Gujarat, within the graveyard communities of Bosnia and Kosovo, within the continuing conflicts and smouldering ruins in Syria ...

During the period of devastation following the tsunami in 2003, the Sri Lankan Christian Council urged the people of the churches to meditate on Psalm 46: '*Therefore we will not fear, though the earth should change, though the mountains shake in the heart of the sea; though its waters roar and foam, though the mountains tremble with its tumult ...*' (NRSV)

Our testimony is to the Spirit brooding within the world's chaos, creating, forming, wooing and calling into being; to the providing of 'bread enough for the day', sustaining, nourishing 'manna', strengthening the journey of the pilgrim community into an unknown future; to the mystery of holding, of being held, held but not protected within the hands of God.

Our testimony is to God's Spirit renewing within the glory and tragedy of the world we inhabit, within each and every human being, whoever we are, whatever we believe or don't believe, whatever we have done for good or ill.

Prayer includes paying attention to God: '*God's giving of God's very self within the membranes of life.*'[5] Our testimony is that we may trust the goodness of God in all things even when God seems so absent.

Discernment belongs to our seeing into the heart of things. I recall an old priest wondering out loud and asking, 'What is God up to within the trauma of Kosovo and Bosnia?' We live within such questions: where is God's life-giving Spirit to be found in the wonder and the terror of the world we inhabit? Where is God's life-giving Spirit to be found within the stuff of our own story? These things belong to a much-neglected way of discernment.

Some will be familiar with the reflective questions for the close of the day in the Ignatian practice of Examen: Where in the day that now comes to a close have I experienced that which is life-giving? ... Where have I experienced that which has closed me down, deadened and switched me off? ... Where have those thresholds been that could lead us through death to life? ...

Discernment can be placed in a different context. A friend spoke of her religious order living through a period of profound transition. Her own work included travelling around the world and country reviewing with others issues of identity, buildings belonging to the Order, personnel, and asking 'Whither now and with what?' She speaks of the importance of watching and waiting within *'the end times, the end of familiar institutions, organisations, religious, educational and social, and the need to help them to die well'*. Also, the importance of waiting and watching for the birthings, for the new emerging patterns and forms belonging to resurrection.

Discernment also belongs within a wider social and political context. On a visit to a number of Caribbean islands in 1982 I asked, 'Who are your prophets? What are they saying and what is happening to them?' The response in each island produced the same name: Allan Kirton, the General Secretary of the Caribbean Council of Churches, a man who spoke out clearly at the time of the invasion of Grenada by the United States. And in the speaking out Allan was called into the government office in Bridgetown, Barbados. The requirement was that he should be silent. Later some members of the churches banned Allan from preaching in their pulpits.

The same questions when asked in Britain continue to produce a strange silence.

Prophecy, I believe, is about discernment: seeing clearly what is happening in society, perhaps too clearly for comfort, seeing beneath the surface of events, seeing through illusions and phoney claims, showing forth what some will prefer to keep hidden. Prophecy is about expressing an anguish that must not be suppressed or denied, in order that the deaf can hear. Prophecy is about public signs, disturbing and offending, requiring attention, response and decision. Prophecy is about the discernment and celebration of the signs of the new creation within the travail of the old.

In conclusion, our work of discernment and of companionship, accompaniment, brings us into the context of the search for meaning, for purpose, the search for a way that is more than expedient, a turning into a future that could be quite different from that which we want or plan. Our work of discernment has to do with paying attention to the nudgings, stirrings, birthing within the life of God's Spirit both in the life of the world and also in our own human stories.

Leave this chanting and singing and telling of beads!

Whom dost thou worship in this lonely dark corner of a temple with doors all shut?

Open thine eyes and see thy God is not before thee!
He is there where the tiller is tilling the hard ground
and where the pathmaker is breaking stones.
He is with them in sun and in shower,
and his garment is covered with dust.
Put off thy holy mantle and even like him
come down on the dusty soil!
Deliverance?
Where is this deliverance to be found?
Our master himself has joyfully taken upon him
the bonds of creation;

he is bound with us all for ever.
Come out of thy meditations
  and leave aside thy flowers and incense!
What harm is there if thy clothes become tattered and stained?
Meet him and stand by him in toil and in sweat of thy brow.[6]

'*God's eternal presence means that God is always fully present in every moment; God is not time-bound – God is. Nor is God space-bound. God is the God of compassion. Consequently, there is no place within our own lives, no height or depth, no length or breadth of our inner states of fear, or terror, of light or of darkness, where God is not, always closer to us than we are to ourselves and always beckoning us to take the leap of entrusting our whole being to the God for whom our hearts are created.*'[7]

Notes:

1. *Honest to God*, John Robinson, SCM Press, 1963. Used by permission of SCM Press/Hymns Ancient & Modern Ltd

2. *Where Three Ways Meet: Last Essays and Sermons*, John Robinson, SCM Press, 1987. Used by permission of SCM Press/Hymns Ancient & Modern Ltd

3. *Between Cross and Resurrection: A Theology of Holy Saturday*, by Alan E. Lewis, William B Eerdmans Publishing Company, 2003

4. From 'Immortal, Invisible, God Only Wise', by Walter Chalmers Smith, from *Singing the Faith*, Canterbury Press, 2011

5. Archbishop Basil Hume, source unknown

6. From 'The Gitanjali', by Rabindranath Tagore (1861-1941)

7. © Gerard W Hughes, 2014, from *Cry of Wonder*, Continuum Publishing, an imprint of Bloomsbury Publishing Plc, p.235. Used by permission of the publisher

A search for identity, living with adoption

A search for identity, living with adoption

Who is this for? It is for those of us learning to live and grow within the implications of adoption, and also for those learning what it means to let go, to hand ourselves over into the unknown.

> 'In the United Kingdom there are at least half a million women who have given up a child for adoption. It is generally agreed that there are around 750,000 adopted people in the country, ranging from the very young to the very old. Half a million birth mothers is therefore a conservative estimate, and many people quote higher figures of 600,000 and more. On these estimates, we calculate that roughly one woman in twenty-five in the population has had a child adopted. The proportion will be even higher for older women, for the number of children adopted was greater when they were young and of childbearing age.'[1]

I am an adopted person and for much of my life have lived without a vocabulary for an inner world of unknowing fed by fear and fantasy, lived with aloneness within the warmth of human belonging. My journey into the search for my birth parents began when I was in my mid-fifties. I was helped not only by close family and friends but also by a social worker from Barnardo's skilled in working with those who live with the implications of adoption. I found my inner voice, discovered a solidarity of understanding, glimpsed fragments of a story I will never fully know. I wrote of this transformative journey in my journal jottings. Here I want to share experiences of unrepeatable wonder and a new solidarity in the search for identity, in living with not knowing, through a variety of reflections and a poem. I have only written three or four poems in my life and am learning that sometimes poetry is the only form available to express what is most necessary.

I hope what I have written will provide encouragement and hope for those who have lived too long with hidden, unshared stories. It may be difficult for those who have no experience of adoption to understand that there are fantasies and fears, imaginings that will not go away and a questioning that increases.

There are children, young people and adults all over the world who, for one reason or another, also are separated from their birth parents, birth families. We all live with not knowing. We all inhabit an inner world for which we have no vocabulary. Sometimes we glimpse our story.

And I said to him
Are there answers to all of this?
And he said
The answer is in a story
and the story is being told.

And I said
But there is so much pain
And she answered, plainly,
Pain will happen.

Then I said
Will I ever find meaning?
And they said
You will find meaning
Where you give meaning.

The answer is in the story
And the story isn't finished.[2]

Notes:

1. From *Half a Million Women: Mothers Who Lose Their Children by Adoption*, by David Howe, Phillida Sawbridge, Diana Hinings, Penguin Books, 1992, p.3. Used by permission of David Howe and PAC-UK (formerly Post-Adoption Centre)

2. 'Narrative Theology 1' from *Readings from The Book of Exile*, by Pádraig Ó Tuama, is © Pádraig Ó Tuama 2012. Used by permission. rights@hymnsam.co.uk

Living with not knowing, holding and being held

This was the first occasion on which I found my voice in public as one who has been adopted. I was invited to give the address at the 'Service of thanksgiving, reconciliation and hope for those living with the implications of adoption', the first of such occasions at a national level, in Coventry Cathedral, on Mothering Sunday, 14th March, 1999.

The Precentor of the cathedral sat with those of us who carefully prepared the liturgy months before, aware of the poignancy of our responsibility.

Within that huge and awesome cathedral there were moments of great intimacy. One such was the invitation to light a candle for a missing person in our lives. I was not alone in wondering if anyone would make that long journey down the aisle to the altar; it began slowly and became a flow. Who were these children walking alone, these women and men of different ages, of different religions and of no religion? What hidden stories lay buried within their blurred gaze? I was not alone in experiencing this day as transformative.

Here are the words I found and spoke into that huge place and sea of unknown faces:

This cathedral in Coventry is such a huge public place for us to come bringing with us what, for most of us, remains essentially hidden within the story of our lives. We will begin by entering the quietness of this place …

Two things by way of introduction:

I speak to you from the comfort of this wonderful Norwegian gravity chair not because I am lazy nor because I want to create a cosy fireside atmosphere. Over the past seven years I have lived with a serious spinal condition necessitating three major operations. This chair has become a friend. It holds and supports and helps in the management of pain. It gives confidence to 'go for things' such as today! I am aware that it may not be easy for you to see and hear and I ask for your patience.

And second: My name is Donald. My birth name was Robert Peter. I was adopted in July 1939 when I was four months old. My younger adopted brother and I have been well-blessed both in our adopting parents and through what has become a wonderful wider family. We were told, simply and lovingly, before commencing school that we were both adopted. There was no real information about our origins and for many, perhaps too many, years no more conversation. That is how it was then. It's different now and I am glad. As with some of you, there have been fantasies and fears, imaginings that do not go away, and a questioning that increases.

A few years ago, during one of the long periods of convalescence, I made my decision to search for my birth mother. The inner and outer journeys were both exhilarating and terrifying. I learned that in the facing of fears some inner healing can come. With the help of others 'a fat file' was discovered, including correspondence from my birth mother. Months later I learned that both parents are dead.

Among us today are birth mothers, perhaps birth fathers, adopting parents, adopted people and family and friends who live with the implications of adoption. Each story is different. What brought us here is different. Most of us, however, have at least one thing in common. We struggle for words to describe our complex inner world. Sometimes it feels like an underground river flowing within us, currents and whirlpools drawing us into places we'd prefer not to go to and shaping us in ways that we don't yet understand.

Most of us have never attended an occasion such as this. That is so also for me. This is the first time I have ever been asked to find words that can be said in public addressing what lies at the core of our experience as people living with the implications of adoption.

I am learning that there are painful yet wondrous gifts to be received through the adoption process and I want to risk beginning to explore two particular areas, hoping there will be some echoes in your experience.

I want to speak of 'living with not knowing'.

Understandably most of us still find it very hard to receive and to accept 'not knowing' as an unwelcome yet profound gift.

At the core of my existence there lies what I can only call 'a dark hole of unknowing', and yet within the unknowing, a knowing. And this is not easily explained! Each of us has lived with 'not knowing'. Where, among all the faces in a too crowded world, is the face of the person once carried in the womb, the one entrusted into the hands of others? How can the silence and aloneness of 'not knowing' continue to be borne? Who is this child, the child entrusted to adopting parents, the loved child, 'our child and yet not our child'? Who is my mother? What pressures within circumstances made it necessary for her to give away her child? Where is she now? Who is my father, lost in the shadows but growing in significance?

Most of us find it hard to live with the bewildering gift of 'not knowing'. There is a deep longing to know, and yet, also a terror of what may be found, of what could be made known.

I wonder if there are some questions that must remain questions, some secrets that can remain hidden, some knowing that we don't need to know, and if somehow, someday we may learn to live with them! Maria Rainer Rilke writes: '*Be patient toward all that is unresolved in your heart and try to love the questions themselves … Do not seek the answers, which cannot be given to you because you would not be able to live with them. And the point is, to live everything. Live the questions now.*'[1]

Perhaps the sense of mystery lying at the heart both of human experience and of creation could become one of those painful and wondrous gifts we inherit. Michael Mayne writes, *'Faith is not about absolute certainty, but a readiness to explore mystery. It is not a method of finding all the answers, but of living with the questions.'*[2]

And yet some of you know, as I now know too, some inner healing can only come through our searching – an endless exhausting searching through records, a searching through fearsome terrains in human experience, a searching within the strange synchronicity of time for a knowing that mysteriously makes itself known.

For me the most profound gift of living with 'not knowing' has been to enter the paradox of the unknowable God whose nature it is to continue to make God's self known within life and through love, a knowing within an unknowing.

I want to speak of 'the holding'.

Most of us, I guess, are still on the edge of what 'the holding' can mean. There is, I am learning, 'a holding' that engenders a trusting, and a trusting that permits a letting go.

Can words ever tell what it means for a birth mother to hold her child, to hold and to trust, to let go and to entrust, to let go and yet to continue to hold in the inner cave of her being, a letting go that is not a forgetting but rather a different way of holding? Can words ever tell what it means for adopting parents to hold and to nurture the child they receive, the child whose nature, whose genes they do not share? There is a holding and watching over growing adopted children who can be so different, in appearance, in temperament, in the worlds they choose to inhabit, so different, yet sometimes knowing a bonding that is closer than blood. There is a holding and trusting that permits a new letting go to become possible; the entrusted one is let go again; it is a primal letting go that alone permits the returning, and a returning in a different way.

Can words ever tell what it means for those of us who are adopted to be held and not controlled, to be influenced in the process of becoming who we are, influenced but not twisted and shaped into the likeness of someone we cannot be, while searching for roots within our unrootedness, for identity within our silent aloneness? Can words ever tell what it means to learn the holding of our complex inner world, the wild and sullen bits that sometimes take over, the inner feelings for which we have no names, the bottomless sorrow, the unshed tears and the overwhelming rage?

Slowly I am learning that there is 'a holding' that befriends and integrates, embraces and pays attention to those bits of us that we fear and from which we hide, a holding that in time can release a wondrous healing.

I am holding in my hand a beautiful piece of wood carved into the shape of a cross by an old man in West Bromwich. Sometimes these little pieces of wood are offered to those who are dying, people for whom words cease to carry meaning, people who find the letting go much harder than they thought. For some these little pieces of wood become alive, calming wild dreams and those long dark nights when we wait for the dawn. For some these small wooden crosses draw them into a mystery, the mystery of 'the holding' of God, 'the holding' through the trauma of being born through the trauma of dying. There is a short and ancient prayer: *'I hold and am held.'* It bears testimony to the hidden holding of God's love within the texture of our fragility and fragmentation.

> *I have spoken of two things: learning to live with 'not knowing' and of 'the holding and being held'. Both, I believe, can be the painful and wondrous gifts for those who live within the adoption process. And not for us alone!*

And a question in conclusion: Did you pick up the rumour in the passage from Exodus, read to us earlier, that Moses is one of us, and also his unnamed mother, his unnamed father and Pharaoh's daughter?[3] And did you know that the fires can still be kindled, fuelling the journey through a wilderness in the quest for identity within our common humanity?

Notes:

1. *Letters to a Young Poet*, by Rainer Maria Rilke, translated by M.D. Herter Norton. Copyright 1934, 1954, by WW Norton Company, Inc, renewed © 1962, 1982 by M.D. Herter Norton. Used by permission of WW Norton Company, Inc.

2. Michael Mayne. Used by permission of Alison Mayne

3. Exodus 1:15–2:10

A dream and a dream beyond that dream

Who am I?

This belongs to a personal and continuing conversation on identity with Jack, one of our grandsons. The dreams came while staying in a retreat house in North Wales.

I have never before written of these dreams and have only rarely talked about them, however they remain for me among the most significant dreams I have ever had. Where the dreams came from and wherein their deeper meaning lies, I am only slowly beginning to comprehend; however I do know they drew me to the edge of what felt like yet another primal mystery.

The first dream was vivid, dynamic, unexpected and seemed to erupt from deep within my unconscious mind. I dreamt for the very first time of my birth father – a dream releasing within me what felt like an historic volcanic rage. Perhaps it erupted from some suppressed place. Perhaps I was projecting unresolved ignorance, fear and anger onto the man whom I had scarcely begun to imagine, twisting and contorting him out of his humanity. For me this felt like a primal encounter between father and son, a form of initiation into my becoming, in my middle years, a man.

What I recall from those sinister shadows is my roaring at the man I recognised to be the father I had never knowingly met before, hurling accusations like explosives: *'Was it another one-night stand? Did you have sex yet again, and again fade into the night? How many other women have there been? How many of them have carried and borne your children? You're a cruel bastard – a selfish bastard! And anyway, who are you?'* I saw no face, only a threatening form in the dark shadows. No crafted words could ever capture the volcanic eruption within me.

And in the outpouring I grew from being an adopted victim into a man, standing shoulder to shoulder, man to man.

I can't express how deeply that dream shook the foundations of my being. The figure of my birth father had played no conscious part in my childhood dreams, always I wondered about my birth mother: who was she, why did she hand me over, what did that do to her, where is she now, does she still think of me?

And there was more to come.

On the next day in the afternoon I chose to walk alone on the beach below the retreat house. It was a long, long beach with clouds scudding low over the sea, gulls riding the strong winds with such effortless, enviable skill.

It was when I had turned to face and move into the winds that a conversation began both within me and also out loud, a dramatic converse with the man I had met in the shadows of my dream. I remember first looking around and, seeing no other person on the beach, beginning what I have never done before or since – I bellowed into the mounting wind, yelling with all the power within my lungs and from the depths of my being. It felt then and now as being somehow primal. This felt different from the dream yet also a continuation; I was consciously roaring out of the hurting rage which had remained hidden and unacknowledged for so long. Again I hurled accusations, argued, battered against him and into the heart of the gale.

How long this primal encounter lasted I do not know but it continued until the outpouring was almost spent. And on my turning back from whence I had come, I looked down and found at my feet stones, stones that drew me toward them. And among them one stone which I picked up and held in my hand, turning it over and around and marvelling at what seemed to be the image of a long wound; and there was yet more: it carried what looked like stitches woven deep, closing and binding for healing, as a heart broken and tended. I have that broken yet healing stone still and forever close by me now.

There was also another dream, perhaps the following night. It was different in texture: the fury abated, the images fading now yet perhaps equally significant. What language can I borrow?

It was as if I had taken a step into a slowly emerging dawn. The man whom I had encountered and whom I despised for his rough animality, his random sowing of his wild oats, his leaving a woman alone to carry his child, alone to face her horrified family, alone to explain to her friends, alone to enter the terrains first of familial rejection and later utter destitution … I am the son of this man in the shadows, his son, the son of his flesh and blood, carrying his genes. Do I also carry this same gene of rough animality, this cruel wildness?

Wherever the dreams came from and whatever the subsequent inner and outward converse might mean, they came as a profound and painful and cathartic gift, yet another beginning within the rest of my life.

And there has been a turning and accepting within an integration, a holding within me of the reality of both light and dark, of the creative and destructive, the cruel and compassionate, the manipulative and transparent, so many opposites swirling and clashing, paradoxes weaving within who I am.

The search for Joseph,
the father in the shadows

I want to write about identity in the context of the father in the shadows. I hope what I have written will echo with others besides those who live with the implications of adoption.

My experience of the father in the shadows is more complex than I first thought. For personal reasons that will become clear later, I have described this as the search for Joseph. In exploring this theme I want to honour the adopting family whom I know so well and also the birth families of whom I know so little. The questions I live with continue to appear, yet the older I become, the more prone I am to wondering and pondering, to accepting paradoxes and living within the mystery of things. I will interpose within the text some of my wondering, my questioning.

I am the father of two daughters and grandfather to five grand-children. My wife Kerstin is Swedish and so I am called *morfar*, which is Swedish for grandfather on the maternal side. Through the years, I have waited for our grandchildren coming out of school both in Birmingham's Moseley and London's Tower Hamlets. Women and men, young and old, parents and grandparents, people of different cultures and faith backgrounds push bikes and prams through those school gates and gather in the playground. Some of us men choose to stand around the edge alone, while most of the women stand in the middle talking with each other.

I wonder increasingly about the nature and significance of fathering. What do we bring as men which is distinctive to the formation of our children and grandchildren? What could it mean to be 'a real father'? What more has to happen in our society for young men of different cultures to be brought up to cherish their role as fathers?

What can be told of my story? There are stories within the stories and there are parts that I choose to keep private. Some things are not mine to share.

My name is Donald, though my birth name was Robert Peter. I am learning that I am both and I am more. Who I am is still unfolding. I was adopted in July 1939 when I was 4 months old. My younger adopted brother and I have been well-blessed both in our adopting parents and through a wonderful wider family. We have been loved and enabled to love. Before commencing school we were told together that we were both adopted. There was no real information about our origins and for many, perhaps too many, years no more conversation. That's how it was then and it's different now and for this I'm glad.

I have an adopted father who loved both my brother and myself, loved us equally and differently. He walked with us on moors and mountains, awakened within us a love of music, followed us when we played rugby, hockey and cricket, watched over us when we lived through rough times, held us but also let us go. His principle was *'hold on and you may lose them forever; let them go and they will return'*. He encouraged us to remain in the testing places; he spoke with us of intimacy within our humanity and of the deep things in life and death. His words were, *'Don't ever forget that death is natural as is birth and is just as much a beginning of new life.'* He found pride in our becoming who we now are. And of course, he was more, much more.

I have a birth father whose shadow increasingly crosses my path. His is as a watermark, a subterranean image, blurred and unsettling.

A few years ago, during one of three long periods of convalescence following spinal surgery, I made the decision to search for my birth mother. I have lived since childhood with fantasies and fears about the mother I have never known and much later in my life moved into a search not only for information but also for encounter. With the help of others a fat file was eventually discovered. It included correspondence. Months later I learned that both my parents had died, my father in 1963 and my mother in 1975. Many share this particular experience of bereavement and, like me, have, as yet, found no ritual in which to focus such complex grieving.[1]

But what of the man in the shadows who fathered me – but was not a father to me? Who was he? What was the nature of his relationship with the woman who was my mother? The birth certificate provides information about her but nothing, nothing, but a blank space with a line through it where there should be details about my birth father. The fat file urged secrecy around my father's identity. Who was this man needing such protection? What secrets were so important that they had to be withheld? I was curious, frustrated and bewildered.

Later I learned that my birth father was a pilot in the First World War, a fine sportsman, a lover of fast cars, a master builder and also a married man with a family. He was described as *'a man's man'*. And his name was Joseph. What was it like for him to have his son given away, the son that he never knew? Did he also wonder where I was? Who I had become? Would he have liked to know that I also was a sportsman?

It has taken a long time for me to recognise that there had been an idealising of my birth mother and a demonising of my birth father. For reasons I can't easily explain I had never faced the father in the shadows. A few years ago during an eight-day silent retreat, I dreamt for the first time of my birth father – dramatic dreams releasing within me what felt like an historic volcanic rage. Perhaps I had suppressed my fear and anger and projected my unresolved ignorance onto him, twisting him out of his humanity. It was for me an inner and primal encounter between father and son, a confrontation between man and man.

I wonder about male physical sexuality and perhaps this wondering belongs to the gifts of the father in the shadows. I wonder about the living of a gentle and non-patriarchal masculinity, the humanising of our 'rough animality', about a passion which fertilises the desire that lies beyond the heat of acquisitive/invasive desire, and I wonder about the transforming of our flawed humanity.

And what does it mean now to say that I am Joseph's son? How much of his nature belongs to the mystery of who I am now? For good and ill his blood flows through my veins, his genes are in my body. I am his son, he is my father.

Kerstin has her family roots in the forest areas of central Sweden and they stretch back into the 16th century. My family roots are elusive and complicated. I wonder what has been passed on to our daughters and grandchildren from my birth father in physical appearance and through traits of nature. It isn't easy to speak together of these things but we have begun.

Was it coincidence that Doris, a friend in Notting Hill, gave me a print of a famous painting of Joseph, husband to Mary and father to Jesus?[2] Doris grew up in a children's home and never knew her father. (See the poem 'Is this not Joseph's son?', p.86.)

I question if there is such a thing as coincidence. Doris and the painting of Joseph? Our granddaughter is attending a secondary school in the same road in East London as my birth father was born and where he lived his growing years? Our eldest grandson is also called Joseph and naturally works well with wood and with the building of things? These unanticipated, surprising links belong within the meaning of a word we seldom use, the mystery of synchronicity.

I have been nurtured since childhood within a faith based in the Fatherhood of God.

I wonder what I have projected for good and ill onto the face of the silent absent one, the mysterious origin of all our relating, whom some choose to call God. What is the nature of the real fathering of the one beyond our imagining?

My search is still for Joseph, and for more, much more.

In my ageing there has been time to follow where questions may lead and in my unwelcome limitation and stability time to ponder the meaning of things.

Notes:

1. Because of the journey I have made within adoption and my living with a serious spinal condition that has required three major operations, I wonder about the connection between trauma and the effect on the body. I wonder about emotional trauma and body memory and the effect on the physicality of our body. And I wonder about serotonin – about which I know almost nothing save that there are within the juices in the brain chemical neurotransmitters, which can be likened to electrical charges, redirecting neural pathways. And the effect is to change physical activity and emotions. See *Molecules of Emotion: The Science behind Mind-Body Medicine*, by Candace B. Pert, Simon and Schuster, 1997

2. *Christ with Saint Joseph in the Carpenter's Shop*, by Georges de La Tour, circa 1635-40

Is this not Joseph's son?

In some pictures of the Nativity Joseph does not appear; in others he is almost lost in the shadows. I have even heard Joseph described as 'the adopted father' of the child Jesus. What are we saying about Joseph the man, his role as father of his son Jesus?

I am not often moved to write in a poetic form yet on occasions it becomes the only way.

In the shadows, silent, scarcely mentioned,
omitted from the first family pictures,
where are you,
who are you,
why have we lost you?

Old Doris Moon in Notting Hill
gave me a print of Georges de La Tour's
Christ with Saint Joseph in the Carpenter's Shop:
no halos, no angels,
just your form, glimpsed in the darkness.
Your face and his face
lit through flickering light,
a candle in his hand.

Were you as the painting shows,
thick in body frame,
arms like tree trunks,
hands strong yet gentle?
Your face bearded, weather-beaten,
radiant – grief-stained –
a well-lived-in face,
forged through interiority.

Handler of wood, worker with nails,
trusted tradesman, master craftsman of Nazareth.

Mary's man, house-builder,
home-maker, love-maker,
rough, tender, intimate man.

And what of your fathering
throughout those hidden years:
the hand-holding,
the addressing of soul,
the standing in his tracks?

What of your fathering through the awakening:
his rising and falling and rising yet again,
his playfulness,
his stretching out,
his reaching deep,

the knowing and the unknowing,
the painful acquisition of life wisdom,
the fearful learning of where faithfulness could lead?
Did you teach him to grow into calling God 'Abba'?
Did he learn from you the prayer,
'Father, into your hands I commend my spirit'?

Who do you see when you look into the face of your child?
What of the son who has grown beyond you?

Well-earthed Joseph,
can you help us with our rough animality?
Can you father us into being,
a birthing within our complex fragility,
born again into our own resilient humanity?

Dear old Doris Moon,
who never knew her father,
thank you for the gift of Joseph –
father Joseph.

Notes:

Christ with Saint Joseph in the Carpenter's Shop, by Georges de La Tour, was painted circa 1635-40 and hangs in the Louvre.

This poem was first published in *Doing December Differently*, Nicola Slee and Rosie Miles (Eds), Wild Goose Publications, 2006

On returning home after the launch of the book *Chosen: Living with Adoption*

The brief I was given for my contribution to the book Chosen: Living with Adoption[1] *was to write as a grandfather and from this perspective explore how being adopted has influenced the course of my life, and also how my experience of adoption has impacted on my philosophy of life.*

The launch of this book was a transformative day in so many ways; I scarcely have words for them.

This is the writing that tumbled out the following day.

The hall in Goldsmiths, University of London, was packed, almost overflowing – adopted people, birth mothers, birth relatives, adoptive parents, counsellors, friends, children, social work academics and social work students. Most of us arrived as strangers; and who in this sea of faces of all colours was who?

Those of us who were readers arrived early to test our voices and calm our nerves. We were quietly addressed by our first names. Some were young and others older, an age span of between 30 and 77 – Biafran, Jamaican, Sri Lankan, Eritrean, Indian, Spanish, Italian, Irish, English, Scottish, Welsh … All who read from the book were adopted; many were young women in their early thirties to mid-forties. Among the readers an actor, a journalist, a therapist, a nurse, a teacher, a dancer, a stand-up comic and of course many more. Some had written before, spoken in public before and others had done neither before so it was a wobbly first. Some anxiously fingered their bits of paper, others proudly held their copy of the newly published book. Some wept as they read, and all smiled as their bowed heads were lifted into the rising applause.

We read extracts from our prose and poems, and there were nods and the quiet murmuring of 'yes, that's it', and also wincing at the lack of sensitivity in stories of raw and subtle racism. And within the writing an awesome perception and articulation, honesty, pride, beauty and resilience.

There was a liberating mingling in a well-planned interval. And in the closing, a question and answer session, and among the questions: 'Where are the men – only three contributors and one reader? Why is it that among the men who are adopted many choose not to search?'

Why has it been so difficult to find the words for this hugely significant, many layered encounter? For a few hours our silence as the adopted ones was broken, our inner stories were heard, the invisible ones became visible, our past belonged within our present, darkened forms re-emerged, and for this short time we were embraced within a community of understanding. Our tongue-tied-ness was loosened, our lack of vocabulary for our inner world found a voice – articulated with such poignant power, such life wisdom, such beauty. Some with historic low esteem, before our very eyes began to unfold, stand tall, proud, confident, tearful, smiling. Our lifelong inner aloneness, uninterpreted difference, yielded into a mysterious yet almost tangible belonging.

So what will be remembered beyond those few hours? Our belonging, our honesty, authenticity, life wisdom, pride, joy, confidence, vitality, humanity, and more.

And now we return creatively unsettled into the silence, into the hiddenness perhaps, and who knows? Perhaps we have caught a glowing glimpse of our rare identity, heard and also found a voice from and within our depths?

One accompanying older friend, well-travelled in almost every way, observed that the young adopted women, more than half her age, had found within their trauma *'an almost enviable life wisdom, an authenticity'* that she herself has scarcely yet known.

On returning home friends asked, 'So how was the launch?' *'Awesome'* has been the one word summary. Perhaps I am still living within an inarticulate creative unsettledness.

So where from here? And also: will there be more such gatherings? I don't yet know, but probably it is a 'no' to more gatherings of this nature: this was a launch, a one-off. We are set free now to fly.

However there are stirrings within me, the old campaigner. I want to seize the moment, get 'the book' out there with pride and hope, far and wide. I belong to those who have 'come out' as adopted, with so much to be thankful for within so much inner pain. I want to seek out adopted men who also live with unresolved questions and encourage them as best I can. I want to keep pushing doors open for adopting parents and for adopted persons, who need safe spaces to take the unsafe feelings and explorations.

Within my physical limitation and ageing I want for others some of the good fortune that has resourced my own 'coming through'.

Note:

1. *Chosen: Living with Adoption* (edited by Perlita Harris) 'brings together writing and poetry by over 50 UK adopted adults born between 1934 and 1984. Through a broad range of perspectives ... they capture the life-changing power of adoption and the different meanings it can take on at different stages in one's life. The themes of identity and belonging, loss and grief, roots and searching, family and 'post-reunion' relationships permeate these first-hand accounts of adoption, as does the power of acceptance and healing, encouragement and hope, and taking responsibility for the direction one's life takes, whatever one's beginnings. Together the writers add to our understanding of the lifelong impact of adoption, offering the reader a wealth of insights and wisdom, together with advice for adopted people and contemporary parents.'

Available from: CoramBAAF, Coram Campus, 41 Brunswick Square, London, WC1N 1AZ, https://corambaaf.org.uk

The body,
wonder and pain:
glimpses of transformation

The body, wonder and pain: glimpses of transformation

I remain in the foothills of transformation.

For much of my life I have taken my body for granted. In my youth I played both cricket and hockey for Yorkshire public school teams, was competitive by nature in tennis, table tennis, badminton, volleyball and swimming, played football in a very physical way for the college team, loved to walk in the mountains, kept fit through jogging, and through most of my adult life, and to my shame, worked all hours. In 1993 both Kerstin and I were brought into an experience of life that we could not have anticipated. It began with my having a series of three spinal operations, and in more recent years, a bypass on my left leg, and being hospitalised with pneumonia. These experiences have drawn me into the depths; life has also cracked open. Kerstin, meanwhile, was made redundant from her post as head of a language development base in one of Birmingham's secondary schools. Her whole life has been reordered. Many continue to ask Kerstin, 'How is Donald?', while only the few ask, 'How are you, Kerstin?'

'There will be new companions,' a wise old friend promised. And to my great surprise and joy this has been true. I have met wonderful people I never knew existed and have encountered prophetic communities. There have been mentors who have become friends. They have helped me to reclaim my body; drawn me into the path of mindfulness and body awareness; reminded me that *'we are wondrously made'*; urged me to listen to and be gentle with my body; quietly and directly asked the unasked questions; explored with me the memory of the body stored in muscles, bones and nerves; helped me to relearn the primal art of breathing; encouraged me on the bumpy path from resignation to reconciliation; helped me to embrace pain and learn through it; told me that I think too much and need to learn to 'go with the flow'; drawn me into the complex paradox of strength and weakness.

Who are these mentors who have become companions, friends? Some, but not all, will be named in the pages that follow: physiotherapists, district nurses, a doctor, a teacher of yoga, an acupuncturist, and also the many who learn body wisdom not by choice but through necessity.

I have said before that writing has become one of my ways of accepting and integrating what is going on around and within me. At times it has become so necessary it is as though something wants to be born. These reflections are drawn from my almost indecipherable jottings scribbled sometimes in the middle of the night, or while waiting in an outpatient clinic or lying in a hospital ward. What I write includes that which is intensely personal and I have wondered if it should be shared. In doing so my hope is that we may encourage each other to be more open in our shared journey into the depths of humanity.

A shocking communion linking us with the crucified and rising body of Christ in all humanity

Countless millions within our human family are born into the community of the world's pain-bearers; they live with relentless poverty and disease, with environmental poisoning, with hurricane and tsunami, with the traumas of war. They have little, if any, access to orthopaedic hospitals, physiotherapists, medication and mental health workers to help them endure their physical and psychological pain. My own journey with my body has scarcely begun to make the connections into this wider solidarity. I write as a Christian who is becoming conscious of a communion that lies beyond the traditional images of the body of Christ in the institutional church, a bodily communion that mysteriously, shockingly links us with the crucified and rising body of Christ in all humanity.

Glimpses of transformation

I want to share encounters within the experience of the new solidarity; reflections on what it could mean to embrace our wounds;
what helps us to manage our interlinking experiences of physical
and emotional pain. They have become for me the rough and tender
terrain within which I have caught glimpses of transformation.

Discovering community, an unexpected solidarity

'*Learning to read the text of the illness … doesn't provide any magical cures. But it does give you a way to perceive Presence within illness and to discover community in the process.*'[1]

A communion beyond a Communion, an unanticipated Pentecost

Writing from my journal, June 2011 and 2014

Did it begin when I fell as I stretched for a book while half-standing on a chair, leaving me writhing in pain on the floor, unable to move save only to reach for my mobile to call for help?

A few days later, in the dark night between Saturday and Sunday morning, and during the weekend when Christians celebrate the Feast of Pentecost, Kerstin drove me to an out of hours clinic in the backstreets of Selly Oak, where I was examined around 3:30am. The doctor phoned the Vascular Unit in the hospital, and immediately we were directed to the Accident and Emergency Department. A few hours later I was in the operating theatre, the surgeon trying to restore the flow of blood in my leg to save it from amputation and performing an emergency bypass leading to a fasciotomy, which left a long wound in my left leg, which remained open for nearly four months of waiting within a slow healing process.

Life had cracked open, yet again. During the eight days on the ward there was a profound realigning experience. Two of the patients were almost blind; the other arrived in the middle of the night for a kidney transplant. I was the one who nearly lost his leg and who began the long wait with an open wound.

In time we began to discover each other, share our stories. It was within our fear and laughter, the shit and awe, the insecurity and fragility, the anger and gratitude that I awakened to a sense that this is the terrain and context of the life-giving and transforming Spirit of the Eternal One. Strangers became intimate friends. The nurses, surgeons and registrars came from every corner of the world. The Queen Elizabeth Hospital in Selly Oak is where the wounded are brought from war zones.

It was Pentecost and the woman chaplain offered all four of us who were patients 'a Pentecost Communion'. My three compatriots all declined and I landed up behind screens. It felt like a 'health and safety Eucharist' in which no wine was offered, just wafers for bread. Inwardly I raged – how can there be no symbol of the 'life-giving blood' present in a hospital where the transforming of our lives was dependent on the blood of others surging through our endangered limbs?

On leaving hospital district nurses tended my wounds at home. They led me through an experience of the mysterious healing processes within the human body in a way I have never known before. In our conversations I discovered that some of the nurses had left churches where they felt oppressed by doctrines and teachings which undermined their own integrity of enquiry and thoughtfulness, their experience of what it is to be an authentic human being. Lying here had been scary and wondrous, a threshold of disclosure. These terrains belong to that which is 'holy ground'.

During these weeks I was drawn to re-read the story of Hagar (Genesis 16 and 21), the Egyptian slave woman driven into the wilderness by Sarah and Abraham, who discovered, as she cried toward God for her child, a spring of water at her feet. The story deepened my wondering about the significance of Hagar, and not only in Islam. What could a Hagar Eucharist look like?

Companions are given not chosen:
a communion of lopsided saints [2]

It has been my experience that hospital wards can be places of learning and transformation. In August 2014 I was in hospital again. We had only been home a few days following our weeks by the lakeside near Kerstin's home village in Sweden when I became unwell, wobbly and began loosing balance. Later, while resting on our bed, I was violently sick, and from then on I can scarcely remember anything. I've been told that I had a high temperature, became delirious and began to speak in Swedish!

I need to write about the community I was drawn into when I was a patient on a ward for those living with delirium and dementia. The journey there was via ambulance, Accident and Emergency Department, the Clinical Decisions Unit and then into the ward. The reason for occupying a bed was pneumonia including delirium. I looked around at my three fellow patients, hoping for a welcoming nod, an understanding smile and there was not a flicker of acknowledgement. In time I learned their names, glimpsed into their unfamiliar worlds. Peter lay snoring, arms 'spreadeagled', mouth wide open, chest rattling, wheezing. It was Peter who caused panic at midnight by sitting up in bed and lighting a cigarette – the ward Sister and her nurses arriving as if there had been a terrorist attack. John in the bed opposite me lay most of the time hunched up in the foetal position, silent save for an occasional violent 'fuck off', 'leave me alone', 'you cheeky bastard'. Rob was my immediate neighbour and nodded in apparent agreement with John's sentiments, his face bearded, shaggy, attentive and at times wild. Rob sat still in his chair but sometimes jackknifed from his bed with scary speed, sparring in verbal combat with his 'friend come to support him', one in a team of mental health carers designated to 'keep close' 24 hours a day. Companions are given not chosen.

My emotions were a cauldron of shock, confusion, disappointment, frustration, fear … I was angry and resented being in hospital only three days after arriving home, following six restorative
weeks by the lakeside in Sweden. And the loo – where someone
had peed around, but not into, the chamber – was rendered a
stinking, wet mess. From across the corridor – in what I imagined
was a private room with fantastic views – a continuous wave of
recorded evangelical choruses was accompanied by a devout,
singing patient. I felt invaded.

I wonder about community, communion and sacrament. In time,
and not through thinking, something dislodged, shifted within me.
This ward of four patients with nurses coming and going is my
given community, the context of communion, the sacred place.
This is the place of holding, being fed, being in relationship,
enlightenment; I became surprised by an inner acceptance.

As Sunday approached I wondered if an invitation to attend the
hospital chapel would come, or an offer from the chaplain to bring
the Eucharist to the bedside behind closed screens. I wondered
about the roots of my increasing ambivalence. Mercifully, I am
embarrassed to say, those offers never came. In a personal letter
Gerry Hughes wrote of our sacraments being celebrations of our
awareness of God at work in all things, in all people and of this
being a continuous reality. A few months before he died, Gerry
wrote another letter and this time about the sacrament of the present moment and his own rejoicing in it. '*I also keep thanking God
for showing me God's presence at work in so many people.*'

There were other offers.

A young doctor invited me to be part of a university research programme, 'Delirium in General Hospital as a marker of undiag-
nosed dementia'. He spoke of his particular project: 'Frailty and
being alive'.

A nurse, young in appearance, while taking a sample of my blood, told of her five children, 9, 7, 5 and twins aged 2, of her husband who is a car mechanic, and of her mother who 'makes everything possible'. She spoke of her Jamaican roots and how the wafting of the choruses across the corridor lifted her soul.

One of Rob's carers, whose origins were in Nigeria, asked each of us: 'Do you believe in prayer?' 'Yes,' each of us replied. 'That surprises me,' he said. 'God offers what God wants through everything and everywhere,' was my clumsy testimony.

There were two Muslim nurses. One told of working as a nurse in the hospital on Sundays and through the nurse bank five days a week; some of her children also work in the hospital. On seeing my copy of the book *I Am Malala*, the other Muslim nurse said, 'She is a brave young woman.' Then she spoke of her own 'standing up' against the prejudices of her wider family and also of her wanting to be a nurse in her culture. Her parents supported her 'all the way' and she resisted wider pressures. A young nursing assistant asked John, following a tirade of swear words, 'John, do you want me to feed you?' 'Yes,' he replied faintly. She attended to him with such respect, naturalness, normality, warmth.

There was a noisy night when my neighbour Rob was especially restless, wandering around, standing and gazing at us from the end of our beds. John had uttered one of his occasional poignant cries: 'Hallo, is there anyone there?' as if seeking assurance there was someone present and listening. Quietly Rob, followed by his carer, crossed the ward, gently stroked John's cheek, then sat still in the chair next to him for nearly an hour. Rob also came to my assistance when I was having difficulty getting out of my special chair. Later I thanked him for having 'pulled me out' of the chair. Thoughtfully he shook his head. 'Not pulled but helped out of the chair,' he said unsmiling.

On Saturday afternoon our minister brought Scots pancakes from 'a thanksgiving party' to be shared on the ward – Scots pancakes with apricot jam, like those we share in our Pain and Hope Group at church. It was through the people on that ward that I was offered community, communion and an encounter with the sacred. A friend described it as '*a communion of lopsided saints*'.

On returning home from the ward there was a swirling carousel of thoughts, feelings, liberation, shock, and a realignment.

Notes:

1. *Broken Body, Healing Spirit: Lectio Divina and Living with Illness*, by Mary C. Earle, Morehouse Publishing, 2003. Used by permission of Church Publishing Incorporated.

2. Some of the names in this reflection have been changed.

Scars and scar tissue

Writing emerging through Holy Week, 2014

'*Our physical wounds never entirely heal, though they may seem to, and we may for a time forget them. Wounds and disease always leave behind recognisable signs: a scar, a characteristic way of walking, a minute change in the immune system or retina that the skilled eye can read, above all what is written on the human face.*'[1]

I don't find this easy to share and trust you have understanding.

A few weeks ago Merlin, the man who continues to treat my spine and the pain in my body, told me of the visit of an Australian acupuncturist who specialises in working with scars and scar tissue. He 'just happened' to be in Birmingham over the Easter weekend and was to lead a workshop for colleagues interested in this area of work. In short, I was invited to meet him on Good Friday afternoon for him to examine my scars. On Saturday, he would treat the scars of a number of patients, including mine.

The scars on my body are numerous: a fall as a child and stitches in my forehead; an operation following an accident in the school gym in which I broke my right ankle during my first season in the school cricket team; three spinal operations between 1993-6 (two in my back and the third via the stomach area in order to secure movement in the implanted scaffolding); the long scar in my left leg and three medium-length scars in my thigh during the bypass and fasciotomy, permitting blood to flow freely again into my endangered foot. Side effects of the third spinal operation emerged from the removal and replacement of my intestines in order to work on my spine from the front of my body. It was an upheaval of nerves, muscles and glory knows what else. The subsequent implications have not been easy to live with.

This has been a mysterious period of synchronism: the examination of scars on Good Friday afternoon and the treatment into the Saturday.

The Good Friday of Holy Week

I will always be grateful to those who have helped me to make the connection between the body of Jesus and our own human body.

The examination.

I need more time to absorb the significance of these days; perhaps I am unwise even to seek the words. It's been strangely 'Galilean' and I didn't expect or perhaps want that to be the case.

Phil the acupuncturist was not what I expected but rather was tubby, jovial, business-like, acutely focused, spiritual in a way I am not used to. He had already read my medical documents. He began with few words, searched for and found the scars on my body and in a very matter-of-fact way. Almost immediately he became animated in the context of the long and wide scar on my left leg, the medium-sized scars and also the blue colour of my foot. He began to treat the scars, and within a matter of minutes the blue of the foot began to change. What he did and what it means I don't know.

I have always been cautious of 'healers' and those who press to lay hands on us but this was different in ways that I must seek words for.

The time with Phil was not as scheduled; instead of the anticipated thirty minutes it became one hour and forty-five minutes. He also worked with the scar marking the spinal operation through the front of my body and which necessitated the temporary relocation of my intestines. Again he became both animated and gentle. He was, I sensed, concerned at what he was finding. He told me that when the intestines are returned they have to form 'fresh bridges to hang on to' and this involved scar tissue clustering, knotting. His was an unusual treatment with spasms running up and down my spine, not sickening, shocking spasms, more wispy! He used language and imagery I am unfamiliar with but later he explained the unknotting, unravelling, unfolding process.

Phil asked for my words in order to provide him with some feedback. So, '... *release, tingling, zapping, wispy spasms, freeing, calming, unfolding ...*' He was eager to learn how the coming night would be and the morning to follow. I slept deeply, that is, until the zinging in my spine began around 4am – but I slept! I slept on my left-hand side with comfort for the first time in years. When I got out of bed I unfolded into a different stretching into my height. The new colouring of my formerly blue left foot was a shock to our daughter at breakfast time.

The Saturday of Holy Week

The treatment was to take place in the presence of approximately twenty acupuncturists who had come both to observe and also 'to lay hands on the pulse'. I was not to be the only one; there were a number of patients with scars.

They assembled and began at 9:00am in a village hall in Meriden, four treatment beds positioned for those of us who were patients, coming and going. I was scheduled for 3:00pm and, after being prepared for treatment, was introduced at 3:05pm. The entourage of acupuncturists gathering around the bed included people of different ages and cultures. Phil asked me to share what I wanted concerning the story of the scars.

It could be likened to a master class. Phil was more than a performer, a teacher ... he modelled a way of being with the patient: respectful, attentive, always beginning with consideration for the patient. It was more than a ward-round with a posse of eager young registrars. He taught not by doing it for everyone to see but rather by inviting colleagues to see what was happening and to wonder, and to seek the evidence. Lots of those who were in attendance wanted to feel my pulse, and it felt different to a 'laying-on of hands' yet also sacred.

Of the other patients brought to see Phil, some had already left while others lingered, each accompanied by their acupuncturist.

This is not the time to wonder what was happening, what this means, where the connections are. Something was happening which I don't understand and that is OK, surprisingly so for one who has been more than sceptical about such things in the past. There was a gentleness, openness, attentiveness, respect, compassion ...

Note:

1. *Pillars of Flame: Power, Priesthood and Spiritual Maturity*, Maggie Ross, Seabury Books, 2007, p.xviii. Used by permission of Church Publishing Incorporated

Wounds and blessings, a search for meaning

The importance of our wounds lies in how we choose to relate to them, how we choose to enter and to integrate them into our lives, for ultimately this integration becomes part of the choice for or against the process of transfiguration. [1]

This writing began in the form of a letter to a friend, one of six letters which I named my 'free flow letters'. They belong in 'Donald's sandpit', a safe place for playfulness within sometimes scary inner terrains.

I want to explore the interconnection between wound and blessing, and by confessing that much within what I write I scarcely understand. Reflection on wounds has been a watermark of much that I have recorded in my personal journals during the past twenty years. I begin by sharing a sequence of circumstances within which this flow of writing was released and also blocked. I intersperse with random wonderings.

The weeping of the body

We came home mid-evening, tired and ready to relax. We watched the first in a series of programmes showing the stories of people involved in adoption: a birth mother looking for the son she gave away, an adopted adult searching for her birth father. I became irritated at what I felt was an emotional exploitation of vulnerable people. Despite how I felt, I became conscious of warm tears trickling down my face, no weeping, no sobbing, just a leaking into a gentle flow. Later I likened the experience to an overflow from a bath too full of water. At the same time I was aware of the familiar 'tidal welling up' within me, both physical and emotional. I say 'familiar' because from time to time and for as long as I can remember, this welling up arises from an unknown source saturating, permeating my being. I have never been able to express this kind of aching in words nor its meaning.

In the years following the third spinal operation we were greatly helped by our family doctor, a woman. During a visit with the intention of seeking more help in managing my body pain, she asked: 'Donald, describe the pain.' And from deep down within me there was an upsurge of tears. 'You are still grieving, Donald,' our doctor said. 'I'm not,' I too quickly retorted. 'You're grieving for the life you once had, the life you might have had.' And I replied defiantly, 'I'm not. I've done that work.' She was right and of course that work remains unfinished.

I wonder what we mean when we speak of 'the body weeping', the image of a sponge, saturated with water, about 'the pain-bearers' who live with the pain of others because they have no choice.

A conversation during treatment

My experience of the welling up of tears was followed by two days and nights of an unusual level of physical pain.

I shared my experience of the tears and the subsequent pain with Merlin, the person whom I visit weekly for the treatment of my spine. He gives me acupuncture and is also a trained counsellor. He has a humble, reassuring, playful way of engaging with the mysterious interlinking of our body and mind. He reminded me of 'the primal wound' within my own personal story as an adopted person, the removal at birth from my mother and being placed in a 'nursery hotel'. Merlin told me that the body has to find a way of managing this trauma, and in time this becomes integrated into our body memory. He also spoke, and here I do not quote verbatim, of a compensating mechanism within the body which may somehow have collapsed within the buckling of my spine in 1993.

On returning home I looked for the book *The Primal Wound*, by the American psychologist Nancy Verrier. It is this book which first provided me with a language and a map for my scary inner landscape. She writes,

> 'What I discovered is what I call the primal wound, a wound which is physical, emotional, psychological, and spiritual, a wound which causes pain so profound as to have been described as cellular by those adoptees who allowed themselves to go that deeply into their pain. I began to understand this wound as having been caused by the separation of the child from his biological mother, the connection to whom seems mystical, mysterious, spiritual and everlasting.' [2]

Wounds within body memory

Bernie, a friend and La Retraite sister, speaks of 'those hidden life wounds, covered by scars yet festering within. When the wounds are touched we howl.' She also points to the possibility of 'our learning to embrace the wounds in such a way that they become part of our greater wholeness, with God's help.'

> I wonder how we are enabled to live creatively and compassionately with our inner wounds and their physical manifestations. I wonder what healing might mean for us within our body memory, and also, who works with such things.

Primal terror

While working on the reflection on adoption 'The father in the shadows', I awoke one morning from a vivid dream. It was of a primal howl across frozen forests. The howl arose from the core of my being. It was a howl of grief, loss and separation and it was the first time I heard such a cry released from within myself. Some of those who have been adopted speak of 'a dark hole of unknowing at the core of our existence'. My howl was from this dark hole toward the silent One.

During the days in hospital following my third spinal operation in 1996, I recall breaking down within a welling up of tears. Mercifully a nurse saw what was happening, and quickly pulled the blinds around the bed. She sat saying nothing, holding my hand, permitting me to seek words for the grief I was experiencing. I was to retire early, aged fifty-six, from work as a minister, leaving familiar networks of colleagues and friends, facing the unknown, symbolised at that time by the promise of 'a life lived in a room'. Within all the grief there was a primal terror of separation, abandonment, loss of identity, aloneness, meaninglessness and probably lots more.

In the years that followed I was accompanied by a Jesuit priest, Gerry Hughes. He helped me to listen compassionately to my primal terror. I entered an emptiness, silence and aloneness which could perhaps be likened in the Christian spiritual tradition to '*the dark night of the soul*'.

Norwyn Denny, my former colleague in the Ecumenical Team Ministry in Notting Hill, became as an older brother for me. Later in his life, following illness and surgery, he wrote of '*the abyss*' as '*the descent into an anguish which comes to most of us at some time or another*'. And of Jesus, he wrote: '*He made of the abyss a road; the place of utter despair, terror, pain and evil becomes a road to bring us nearer God.*'

In my book *Grain in Winter* I began to explore the waiting within unholy Saturday experiences, grief, disappointment, letting go, waiting with no hope.[3] This is the context within which the young American theologian Alan Lewis, while living with terminal cancer, testifies to '*divine fertility*' within the grave, the tomb, the descent into hell.[4]

The blocks

I still need help with the interrelatedness of body, mind and emotions, the psychosomatic nature of who we are.[5] I am learning that my greatest physical pain includes an awareness of a dark whirlpool of emotions, including an angst emerging from my inner world, both conscious and unconscious. I have found this difficult to engage with. And, when I was ready to embark and explore within this terrain, some of those whom I needed to listen found it difficult to engage with. Following a scary period when night pain became too much, I welcomed the offer of the services of a psychologist at the Pain Management Clinic and was assured that an appointment would be made. This never materialised and I chose not to pursue it. This has been the context of one blockage and I still wonder why. There could be others.

Well, perhaps you did not anticipate such a flow within such a blockage.

Three short prayers have become mantras for me:

> *Lord, help us so to embrace our wounds that they become part of our greater wholeness.*

> *Jesus, draw us into your body, risen yet wounded in all the world.*

> *May we discern the marks of resurrection in the wounds we carry.* [6]

Notes:

1. *Pillars of Flame: Power, Priesthood and Spiritual Maturity*, by Maggie Ross, Seabury Books, 2007, p.xviii. Used by permission of Church Publishing Incorporated

2. *The Primal Wound: Understanding the Adopted Child*, by Nancy Newton Verrier, British Association for Adoption and Fostering, 1993, p.xvi. Used by permission of CoramBAAF

3. *Grain in Winter: Reflections for Saturday People*, by Donald Eadie, Epworth Press, 1999

4. *Between Cross and Resurrection: A Theology of Holy Saturday*, by Alan E. Lewis, William B Eerdmans Publishing Co, 2003

5. 'If we accept the idea that peptides and other informational substances are the biochemicals of emotions, their distribution in the body's nerves has all kinds of significance, which Sigmund Freud, were he alive today, would gleefully point out as the molecular confirmation of his theories. The body is the unconscious mind! Repressed traumas caused by overwhelming emotion can be stored in a body part, thereafter affecting our ability to feel that part or even move it. The new work suggests there are almost infinite pathways for the conscious mind to access – and modify – the unconscious mind and the body, and also provides an explanation for a number of phenomena that the emotional theorists have been considering.'

   From *Molecules Of Emotion: The Science behind Mind-Body Medicine*, by Candace B. Pert, Touchstone, 1997, p.141. Used by permission of the Estate of Candace B. Pert

6. Bishop John Austin

Learning to live with pain

None of us likes a world where those we love develop cancer, get Alzheimer's disease, live with MS, have bodies twisted through arthritic pain, where friends are knocked down and killed on the road, where families we care for experience the continuing pain of separation and divorce. We want God to prevent this and to keep life's pains away, and particularly from our family, friends and ourselves.

Some of us, myself included, need to learn to express our rage, bewilderment and anguish toward God in a way that is real. We are not good at this and need to help each other. I was once asked by a doctor in a hospice to help a lady who had suffered for many years to express her anger towards God. Neither she nor I was used to such a suggestion.

We are not promised a rose garden. Nowhere have we been promised that our way through life would be easy. Some pain simply has to be borne and we need help to accept it, to live with it. We need help to manage pain.

Pain is experienced in many forms and is often interconnected. Some of us live with the implications of unexpected and unwanted events that reshape our lives. Many of us live with the wear and tear which comes through our ageing. Pain can frighten, exhaust, wither, depress and isolate us, but also illumine, deepen, mature and draw us into interconnectedness and solidarity with others. Pain has been described as *'a strangled message'*.

We are learning that the Church speaks much of pain and suffering but is embarrassed by it.

The accident,
'Receive the gift of the old man'

(This is an edited version of a contribution to a conference in the Oxford diocese.)

The encounter with the old man lying on the road broke my life open and led into the terrifying terrains of transformation. 'Are you still carrying the old man on your back?'

Some of us live with the implications of unexpected and unwanted events that reshape our lives. I have been slow, perhaps reluctant, to acknowledge the story of pain hidden within my own life story, its interconnectedness within the search for meaning.

I am choosing to share that which is deeply personal. For a short period the impact of these events was very public, and later followed by a great and an almost unbroken silence. For the most part I have chosen not to speak publicly of these things. I share them now hoping that within the unfolding there will be resonances which could lead us into conversation.

Near the conclusion of our ten years living and working within the ecumenical group ministry in Notting Hill, I was appointed to become Tutor in Pastoral Theology at Wesley College in Bristol. As part of my preparation I visited a former Dominican monk who lived in Kent; he worked with me on matters of formation: what it could mean to become 'a man or a woman of God'.

It was on a glorious spring morning in April 1981 that I travelled by car from Notting Hill to Mark Collier's Retreat Centre, south of London. Near to my destination I was involved in a car accident in which an old man in his 90s died.

It was and remains a profound encounter and one which in many ways has changed my life. And some of that is for the good.

I am told that the witnesses at the Coroner's Court reported that I didn't have a chance – I was part of a tragic and bloody encounter that ended a life. I watched over the old man on the road while ambulances and police came; and while people watched from a distance, no one came close, no one. It was then, and for a long time has remained, a nightmare. I was in the mess and not an observer. I was a part and not apart, and for some reason this has also been and remains profoundly important.

Two days after the accident it was Passion Sunday and I was planned to both preach and preside at the Eucharist in morning worship in Notting Hill. I explained to the social worker colleague who was appointed to share in leading worship that I felt unable to take my part. She replied, 'Donald, if you think you can wash your hands clean enough to break bread then you have got things profoundly wrong.'

At the time, I was in what is called a Jungian training analysis, working with the adoption experience. The phrase that was offered to me from those early days after the accident was this: *'Receive the gift of the old man.'*

As I have indicated, through the years I have chosen not to talk about this encounter. I have wanted to, needed to, but not felt able. Some of my closest friends, among them wise and godly people, held back from engaging with the trauma. People want painful things to go away. They want us to put it behind us, forget it. In my experience life isn't like that.

I was, however, permitted to go into the depths through the companionship of two Roman Catholic priests, Michael Hollings and years later Gerry Hughes. In more recent years also through Bernie, a tough and tender La Retraite sister who continues to offer a rare friendship, and who embodies a body wisdom emerging from her own living with a severe spinal condition. With other members of her religious order, Bernie is engaged in a project reflecting on human suffering and love. They are being asked:

'Where is God, or grace, or hope, as you see it, in your encounter with suffering, diminishment or loss?'

In an early session with Bernie I made reference to the trauma experienced through the accident. Her almost immediate response was, 'Donald, are you still carrying the old man on your back?' And yes, I acknowledged that both consciously and unconsciously I was still carrying the old man on my back. She confronted my sense of unresolved guilt, my need for mercy, my wondering what an absolution could look like. 'Sorrow yes, regret yes, shock and horror yes, but not guilt.' And within this conversation she spoke of 'somatosis': the effect of traumatic life experiences within the hidden memory of the human body. [1]

I don't believe the accident caused my spinal condition, but there could be a mysterious interconnectedness.

Ingela, who is a physiotherapist and a member of our family in Sweden, suggested that I find a way of talking about the trauma, and to my surprise suggested that the police could be an obvious first call. So I wrote to Steve, who is a policeman in our congregation. People in the police force experience indescribable events. Steve and I found each other as human beings, listened to each other and at considerable depth. He was able to speak of God to me.

My continuing to carry the old man was symbolised by my keeping the file with my journals written following the accident – the letters, papers, poems, prayers sent during that long period of dazed confusion. Prior to moving house ten years ago Kerstin asked, 'Why are you still carrying the file with you?' On hearing my response she urged that I only get rid of the contents when the time seemed right.

It was on an Ash Wednesday that the contents of the file were burned, ashes scattering and falling onto the awakening spring soil, a simple ritual in the garden of the house belonging to the La Retraite sisters. There were no formal words, just a quiet watching over the fire, the rising and drifting of burned pieces of paper, wisps of smoke.

All was burned save two letters. One was from Sid Millar, Director of the Family Service Unit in Notting Hill, who had loved me enough to be poignantly direct, unnervingly rigorous. He urged that I should not get lost in a guilt that could consume and destroy, a letter that only a true and courageous friend could write. His subsequent visit to our home a few weeks after the accident was brief and quiet. 'This experience can destroy but could also re-create you.' I sensed I was experiencing both. The other letter was from the old man's priest, who wrote, 'We do not raise ourselves, God raises us.'

It was Bernie who helped me through the simple and relaxed ritual in the garden. First I gave her the two letters I had chosen to keep and in the silence she read them. Then she gave me a poem, 'For someone awakening to the trauma of their past', from *Benedictus*, by John O'Donohue. Here are two verses in the poem:

Only you know where the casket of pain is interred.
You will have to scrape through all the layers of covering
And according to your readiness, everything will open.

May you be blessed with a wise and compassionate guide
Who can accompany you through the fear and grief
Until your heart has wept its way to your true self. [2]

I read it in the silence; it continues to move me deeply. I wonder where in the life of the poet those words sprang from.

Later, Bernie spoke of the hidden, perhaps forgotten, wounds in our life, how we trip over them, pick at them. 'There is also the possibility,' she said, 'of embracing the wounds, permitting them to belong to our greater wholeness, with God's help.' This has been the place of profound inner realignment.

What is it in me that remembers, and is haunted by guilt, shame and shock, and forgets those expressions of well-earthed honesty, wisdom, understanding, compassion and grace, including from the old man's family and their priest? We are being held, though we do not know it at the time.

The Notting Hill years were cathartic: I allowed pain to enter my well-walled, protected life, to enter my soul, to inform insights, to illumine the path I walked, to begin the slow work of transformation. The book lying on the floor of the car at the time of the accident, covered with glass, was a newly purchased copy of Martin Israel's *The Pain that Heals*.

Abel Hendricks, a Cape Coloured minister, on the night before leaving us in Notting Hill and returning to apartheid South Africa, spoke of his country as lying in broken fragments, and being gathered into the wounded hands of Christ to be transformed into '*a yet more glorious mosaic*'.

Slowly, and in my imagination, I began to hand over the broken fragments of my life into the wounded hands of Christ, the broken images of myself, of God, the shattered dreams, the false assumptions about strength and weakness, about the nature of wealth and poverty, good and evil, all turned upside down.

For me, the accident reformed expectations of those called to become stewards of the mysteries of God.

> *Who in the world, I continue to wonder, are now the priests and where now in the world are the altars.*

In conclusion two short prayers written by friends:

> *Lord of every pilgrim heart,*
> *bless our journeys*
> *on these roads*
> *we never planned to take*
> *but through your surprising wisdom*
> *discovered we are on.* [3]

Peter Millar

Through fire and water
you have brought us

Through storm and bitter hurt
you have brought us.

Through searing pain and bitter wound
you have brought us.

Through years of searching and of longing
you have brought us.

Day after day, night after night
to this time and place.

With friends and companions
you have brought us.

With searching, discovery and delight
you have brought us.

With pilgrims of age and the laughter of childhood
you have brought us.

With pilgrims of many faiths and of none
you have brought us.

Surrounded by and one with all the saints in light
you have brought us.

Day after day, night after night
to this time and place. [4]

Bill Denning

Notes:

1. See *Molecules of Emotion: The Science behind Mind-Body Medicine*, by Candace B. Pert, Simon & Schuster, 1999

2. From *Benedictus: A Book of Blessings,* by John O'Donohue, published by Bantam Press. Reproduced by permission of The Random House Group Ltd. © 2007 and the Estate of John O'Donohue

3. Peter Millar, from *A Book of Blessings*, Ruth Burgess (Ed.), Wild Goose Publications, 2001. Used by permission

4. Used by permission of Jill Denning. Bill Denning was a creative presence on the edge of the Methodist Church. He lived with Jill, his wife, on a farm which they transformed into a small retreat centre. They had a considerable influence for good on a number of those preparing for ordination. Bill died about 10 years ago.

The muddy path of an older pilgrim

While pain can bring us to a place of exhaustion and isolation, it can also draw us into a community of friendship with those learning to live an authentic body wisdom with humour and a light touch.

On my arrival at church one Sunday morning an elderly lady was making her way slowly to the entrance doors. 'How are you?' I asked. Pausing to catch her breath she replied, 'I am staying with it.' This time it was my turn to pause. 'Staying with what?' I asked. This brief encounter opened up a friendship. What is it that we choose to 'stay with' that is so important for us?

It is, however, about Barrie that I want to write. Barrie was elderly and frail when I first grew to know him, his body exhausted and bent with physical pain, yet his dulled eyes shone with an unassuming life wisdom. I wrote this letter to Clare, his daughter, on hearing of Barrie's death.

Dear Clare,

I need to write about your father and also to find my own way of living with the loss of a friend.

Our home has been in some ways transformed by his one visit. I scarcely knew Barrie when he asked to come, not giving the reasons why. It was a wet day when he came. His appearance was that of a man of great age, frail, stooping, bearing pain both in body and soul, but it was the look in his eyes that struck me most.

I did not have the heart to ask Barrie to take off his shoes, as is our custom on entering our home. I led him slowly up our carpeted stairs to my room with its view of huge trees being transformed again through all their seasonal changes. Slowly Barrie followed me and I made him as comfortable as was possible.

Why did Barrie come? He knew that I also live with pain, physical pain and also the pain of those memories that accumulate in our muscles and nerves through all the years. So that is where we met, with a gentleness and quietness born out of exhaustion. We explored what helps us to manage that which at times feels unmanageable. We were led to the necessary places within us and found the words which were 'good enough' for us.

I will never forget that hour, nor the slow journey down the stairs to the front door and out to his car and the gentle wave of 'farewell'. And that's it. I think we both sensed we had found in each other a quiet, understanding friendship.

Later I discovered the muddy footmarks on the stairs and my heart dropped. In time those marks grew to carry a meaning which I still can't express. I have told so many of Barrie's journey into the room and his leaving what I now call 'the muddy marks of the pilgrim'. Barrie has left a mark in my heart as well as on our carpet. I tell others that they 'tread in the path of an older pilgrim'.

Our mutual friend Vivien is much more than an experienced teacher of yoga. Following Barrie's visit to our home, your mother Eileen, Barrie and I met regularly in the front lounge of their home for what Vivien called our 'Prana group'. She helped us into our breathing exercises, into the mindful re-occupation and befriending of our painful bodies. For us Vivien was as an angel.

Please share this with your family as you see to be helpful.

Peace and love to you, Clare, to Eileen and to your family.

Donald

The Pain and Hope Group

I have been encouraged to 'name the fears'.

Elsewhere I have written concerning my fears in anticipating the transition from my too full, too busy life lived in what I thought to be the centre of things, toward a life symbolised by and lived in the confines of a room. After my third spinal operation I broke down in the hospital ward, wept and wept. I feared the loss of role and identity, leaving familiar networks of relationships, being forgotten, entering a life with no obvious meaning or purpose, disappearing down the plughole of self-pity.

It is not easy to convey the significance in my life of the little group we affectionately grew to call PH7, the Pain and Hope Group. It was a movement out of isolation into community. Nearly always I have come home after our being together buzzing with excitement, wonder and thankfulness.

This has become one of the terrains wherein I catch glimpses of transformation.

The absent present ones

In the beginning it was not my idea but rather that of our minister who, being aware of people experiencing difficulty managing physical pain, suggested we might find encouragement in meeting together. There were a couple of younger women with congenital hip conditions, older people with arthritis and two people with severe spinal conditions. The age range was from mid-thirties to early nineties. At first there were seven of us. We called ourselves PH7.

What happened when first we began to meet all those years ago? We arranged chairs in a circle, including space for two bed-like chairs; we placed a small table in the middle with a lit candle on it; we shared silence; read a poem; took it in turns to 'tell it as it is' with those who listened with a different quality of understanding; we closed with prayer. We met not to grumble or complain but rather to encourage and support each other, to compare strategies and to exchange tips for a variety of our situations, including how to live through a painful night. Always we had an empty chair drawing our attention to 'the absent present ones'.

Following one PH7 session Ron gave each of us a beautifully inscribed copy of a prayer that meant a lot to him, and also now to us:

> *God grant me the serenity*
> *to accept the things that I cannot change,*
> *courage to change those things I can*
> *and wisdom to know the difference.*
> *Amen* [1]

Learning what is ours to accept and discovering what we need not accept is not easy: we need wisdom, courage, compassion for ourselves and also help from others.

We came together with our questions:

What to say when people ask: 'How are you?' …?

What to do with our anger, rage and frustration? …

How to pray in a world inhabited by millions who live with pain caused through wars, earthquakes, tsunamis, environmental poisoning and disease? …

During one PH7 gathering we focused on medication and constipation, such was our spirituality. A few days later each of us received from the 90-year-old member a handwritten list of recommendations for our living with constipation:

1. Eat plenty of roughage (fibre). Oats and oat bran which can be added to any cereals and soups.

2. Also foods with plenty of fibre, including brown rice and beans and most fruits (prunes, raisins, currants) and especially apples – should eat one every day.

3. With extra fibre, you should drink plenty – at least 6 glasses of water a day or fruit juice. Coffee also helps.

4. Exercise is important to keep the bowels supple.

After a few years the life of this first group necessarily and naturally came to a close.

A new group came into being, including five people in wheelchairs, some living with cancer, others with arthritic pain, a person with an acute respiratory condition, another with MS and another with motor neuron disease. Two former nurses with experience in palliative care also belonged to the circle.

We live in a culture where fear is 'out of sight, out of mind'. So we have continued to keep an empty chair as our way of being mindful of 'the absent present ones'. Paying attention to the reasons for their absence becomes part of the agenda; being in touch later in a way that is meaningful belongs to our communion. Most of us, at some stage in our lives, will need to learn to accept our limitations, to withdraw from being present in former ways and learn how to be absent, yet present in other ways.

Since PH7 first came into being a number of the company have died: Ron, Mary, Sue, Jean and Michael. Each of them in their different ways have shown us what it is to live our dying. We remember them, ask after their loved ones; this also belongs within our communion.

Tony is our resident poet. Each time we meet we read one of his poems, often written especially for us. Here are two:

The empty seat

Love draws us here
To a place of hope and pain,
Where hurts and hearts
Are opened up again
To One who holds us
In quiet depths.

The love that binds us
To each other, in the beat
Of the world's great heart,
Is broad and deep and high:
Alive as bread and breath,
Warm as wine.

And so we keep this empty seat,
A space for other places
To be a part of this place,
Reached and touched and held,
Across the separated silence
Of our longing.

Tony McClelland

PH7

We walk lonely ways of pain,
    But here, for a time,
        Our ways, and our stories, cross –
And we recognise
    In each other's eyes
        And words,
The truths we have learned alone:
    The slow wisdom of the body,

The whispered call to waiting.
And discover, all over again,
  The strength we share
  In weakness.
And here, in this between time,
  The threads are woven,
  In permitted silence,
As we step again into solitude, knowing
  Both the light we grasp,
  And the shadow we fear,
Are the cloudy, fiery pillar
Leading us on.

Tony McClelland [2]

Michael and Gordon: the ministry of the disabled

Our recent minister lived with cancer during her time with us and chose to belong to the Pain and Hope Group. She encouraged us to explore ways in which we could bring a service of prayer for healing and wholeness into the worship of the Church.[3] It has taken us a long time in the wider Church to recognise disabled people as those who can minister, rather than as those who are ministered to.

In our church, during the Service of Prayer for Healing and Wholeness, instead of going to the front to kneel and receive the bread and wine, the queues of children and adults make their way to the back of the church, where those in wheelchairs and their carers worship each Sunday.

A plate with the bread was given to Michael and Gordon, both wheelchair users, and they became the ones who looked us in the eyes with the words: *'The body of Christ keep you in eternal life.'* Able-bodied people stood alongside them each offering the cup to us with the words: *'The blood of Christ keep you in eternal life.'* And each of us muttered our 'Amen', our 'Yes, so be it'. For some this was a transforming encounter.

During the two years that Michael lived with motor neuron disease he shared his journey through writing articles. In one he wrote:

> *'Our discipleship is not necessarily a journey from darkness to light, but sometimes seems to move in the opposite direction, from the known to the unknown, from the clear to the unclear. If I try to relate that to my own life I have far more questions now than I ever did at the beginning of my faith journey. In one very real sense I know less than ever about this God who calls me to follow. In another sense the call to make the journey is as real and insistent as ever. I have to be content to let God lead me into an unknown land, even into darkness.'*

I recall a talk Michael gave to a group of trusted friends on what he believed, what he felt, and what he needed, entitled 'The unwanted journey toward death'. I asked him during a visit to their home, 'What shall I say to those who ask how you are?'

His reply was: 'Tell them I am living, I hope, in gratitude and in anticipation.' On another occasion he said that he was having 'a bummer of a day, with constipation'.

During a period of respite in the hospice Michael asked if we could share a period of silence together (he didn't find silence easy on his own). Our silence was broken when a young nurse entered the room. She approached Michael with due respect and whispered into his ear: 'Michael, have your bowels opened today?' I can still hear the laughter.

Michael left us a prayer:

> *Lord, there is such beauty and anguish in your world, beauty and anguish are in your heart. May we be transformed as Christ is through love and anguish. Amen*[4]

Notes:

1. From a longer prayer by Reinhold Niebuhr written in 1934, later adopted and popularised by Alcoholics Anonymous.

2. Tony McClelland poems used by permission of Tony McClelland

3. The 'Order of Service for Healing and Wholeness' from the *Methodist Worship Book* became part of the rich diversity of our regular worship.

4. Michael's words used by permission of Mary Jackson

What helps us in our management of physical and emotional pain and who comes to our aid

The miracle we seek is managing, managing what at times feels unmanageable, with God's help. I thought I knew the stories of Jesus, his testing in the wilderness, his agony in the Garden of Gethsemane while his disciples slept, but for most of my life failed to notice the testimony to the presence of angels ministering to him, strengthening him (Mark 1:12, Luke 22:43). I am now learning that angels come in many forms.

I have not 'got pain sorted' but hope that we can encourage each other to be real, to be honest rather than heroic, straightforward, and eventually find our own strategies.

Often we forget what we have learned; we do mindless things and we pay the consequences. On occasions we face choices and we 'go for it' and we suffer later; also, we learn to spit, grin and sigh, 'But it was worth it!' To describe these journeys as transformative may be an exaggeration but hopefully we catch enough glimpses!

Those closest to us

Kerstin is my wife and in so many ways I have become increasingly dependent on her.

Her life has been reshaped. She carries not only our shopping but also my chairs, hangs the washing, drives the car and cuts my toenails. I was wisely advised not to burden her with an unnecessary recitation of how I am and instead give her a daily 'weather report': enough information for those who ask.

Kerstin watches my stumbling into half-remembered strategies. She knows my nights are interrupted by pain, her first question in the morning being, 'How has the night been?' She watches over me when the tears of the body well up, when frustration breaks into expletives.

Kerstin needs her times away from all this.

Pain management

We seek a management of pain including and beyond those necessary pills. We want to be truly alive.

An invitation to attend the 'Pain Management Clinic' understandably raised our hope. I could write about the experience of the clinic in the 1990s but it is not appropriate to pursue that here. The queue of people wanting help with pain is unending and overwhelming. How the consultants, nurses and physiotherapists sustain their daily attentiveness I do not know.

The surgeon who undertook two of my three spinal operations was more than a doctor for me: he addressed my soul. In the final consultation before he retired he helped both Kerstin and myself to understand the current condition of my spine, and more – he helped me to face and accept my own responsibility in the management of strategies. It was an unexpectedly liberating encounter. 'This is how it is. You have a lot of living to do, so get on with it.'

Acupuncture and moxa

I am one of those who has been slow to respond to the alternative health processes. Intuitively I know whom I trust and whom I regard as phoney.

With reluctance, but with the recommendation of my physiotherapist, I attended an open day at a Back clinic and this was where I met Merlin, who works through acupuncture. He wasn't sure he could help but said he would like to try. He is a qualified counsellor and trained to listen for those hidden life stories within the story of our body. Acupuncture doesn't change the physical reality of having scaffolding in my spine. The treatment sometimes floods my body with calm; mostly it restores within me the ability to manage what at times seems unmanageable. Merlin is a wise, skilled and, in his distinctive way, deeply and authentically spiritual man, for whom the human body is a wondrous mystery. He works largely by touch, assessing what he describes as the 'imbalances' within the human body, then administers treatment intended to restore better balance. For me Merlin is much more than a humble healer: he dares to address the interrelated soul questions. He helps me not only with physical strategies but also with the nature of who I am. 'Donald, aim at 70% of what you want to do and then cut another 10% off!'

Over many years Merlin has increasingly treated me with moxa, a traditional Chinese medicine/therapy which consists of burning dried mugwort on particular parts of the body. This is known to improve circulation and boost the immune system.

With other colleagues Merlin formed Moxafrica, a small charity focused on enabling research into the use of moxa in the treatment of drug-resistant TB. TB is the largest infectious killer in the world today, endemic in populations cursed with poverty. I believe this small Moxafrica team to be a prophetic community.

Managing the subtle inner teasing

There is within us a psychological tease that nags away, whispering that we are frauds: our pain is all in our mind and not in our body.

My friend Bernie, the La Retraite sister, recommended that I obtain through the consultant a copy of the X-ray in which I could see the implanted scaffolding; this has helped in those self-questioning moments. Similarly I keep in my file a letter from the doctor explaining the medical condition. We are not frauds. I also obtained a letter for when we travel abroad, along with a list of the medications I take, just in case I need it in an emergency.

Soul pain

Often we assume that our pain belongs only to the body. I am learning that we may also live with what some describe as 'soul pain'. We may need someone to help us to listen, learn and disentangle within this place.

I have a mantra through which I breathe in and breathe out when I am in a sorry state physically and emotionally. The use of a mantra is not about blocking out, anaesthetising or denying the messages of that pain but rather accepting, befriending, integrating it. 'In your mercy, transform.'

I wonder about the healing of those painful memories that are stored up in the muscles, nerves and tissue of our body.

Bowels and the white bucket

Some may be surprised at the significance I attach to bowel movements and the language I use. I need and want a good daily evacuation yet it rarely happens! So walking, drinking lots of water, a laxative on prescription and Kerstin's wise cooking with fresh vegetables, fruit, fibre, lots of water, all come to our aid, eventually! These things belong to our sense of well-being, and with them the traversing of the night also improves.

The way our body naturally excretes waste out of our system, cleanses it from infections, is a wonder almost beyond our comprehension. I had mini-seminars on these things from the district nurses who kept vigil over the long open wound in my left leg following the bypass, the fasciotomy operation.

I wonder about 'crap' in other interlinked ways. When we are small children we have 'potty training'; we are taught where, when and how to open our bowels, to shit in the right place. I wonder how we clean out the emotional 'crap' in our systems, what belongs to this 'potty training'.

In my room I have a simple white bucket; it was given by a wise and discerning friend during the first of three long periods of convalescence. On opening the parcel I raised an eyebrow, curious as to its purpose. 'There is stuff inside us which left may fester and poison. This bucket is for you to spit in.' By temperament I am not one of those who find it easy to get 'the inner rubbish' out of my system. I suppress it, bottle it, rather than finding a way of symbolically 'binning it'. I am learning to use the white bucket.

A friend, who is a social worker living with huge pressures around and within her, rang our doorbell one lunchtime and asked: 'Can I use your white bucket for 20 minutes?' I took her to my room and left her alone. Later she emerged smiling. 'That feels better,' she said. Each of us must find our own way to deal with the crap, perhaps though art, poetry, music, gardening, running, journal writing, co-counselling or therapy.

Another friend spoke about earth and compost and getting her hands dirty, and finished up talking about 'the crap' that is around and how she can't cope with it. So we looked at compost and crap and where God is in it all. Perhaps we need a theology of compost and crap, we thought – we called it 'shitology'! I'd never thought of 'the crap' quite like that before.

Lament

There is an historic tradition of lament, which is neglected by many within the institutional Churches. Recent terrorist attacks in Manchester and London and the fire raging through Grenfell Tower have shown a deep human need to express bewilderment, grief and rage through bringing flowers to the place of sorrow, where candles are lit, vigil is kept. These places become our new 'portable wailing walls'.

Keeping our body in good condition

I was a sportsman and still am in my heart.

Following the third spinal operation, and with Bernie's recommendation, I was introduced to Shannon, a young American physiotherapist. We paid for her to come to our home. Shannon taught me to walk again and developed a pattern of daily exercises. She gave me my body back, awakened wonder in the miracle that is the human body, restored a sense of physical self-respect and emotional well-being. Shannon also belongs to the humble healers.

A few years later I asked at both the Medical Centre and the Pain Management Clinic for a session with a physiotherapist to review those first daily exercises, but with no success. I was even told at the clinic that a physiotherapist might make things worse through aggravating the spine with the wrong exercises! Later, and through persistence, one of the clinic nurses arranged for me to have an appointment. It was a one-off yet helpful. Periodic review of the daily exercises carries for me a sense of necessity.

Recently I was thoroughly assessed in a hospital physiotherapy department and this led to much more than a revised series of exercises. I had mini-tutorials, one of them being on the complexity of that critical junction of the human body known as our shoulder, and again I was led into a threshold of wonder and gratitude.

Foot massage

Sometimes in our family we give each other a simple foot massage. I prefer to be the one giving the massage but sometimes I receive it and it helps. My feet are very sensitive and foot massage sends all kinds of messages up into my spine.

I am told that foot massage helps to loosen constipation; it is worth having all that helps.

Between the spinal operations Sue, one of my former students, offered to massage my feet. I accepted with reluctance and some embarrassment but am so grateful that I did.

Walking meditation

When I came out of hospital following the final spinal operation, a friend gave me a small book entitled *The Long Road Turns to Joy: A Guide to Walking Meditation*, by Thich Nhat Hanh, a Vietnamese Buddhist monk and Nobel Peace Prize nominee. Walking is more than getting from our home to the local shops and back again. The author gives simple exercises for walking to aid awareness, to increase our mindfulness as to what we can see, smell and hear, to deepen attentiveness within the present moment. It is so simple, basic and helpful.

Semi-supine

I have been helped by what in the Alexander technique is called 'the semi-supine'. It was Bernie who introduced me to the simple practice of lying on my back on the floor, with a thick book under my head, with my knees up and close together, my feet flat and slightly apart, and my hands resting on my ribs, for about twenty minutes. I include this in my resting times most days. How does it help? For me there is a sense of bodily realignment and, at times, a feeling that I can rise and conquer almost anything! For me this simple practice can take place almost anywhere and continues to be profoundly restorative.

The nights

I have been helped to understand why pain increases in the night. The discs either side of the scaffolding in my spine compress during the day while I am standing and walking around the house; while sleeping in the lying position the discs expand, and muscles and nerves are affected.

How to achieve change when the pain is too much? In a word – distractions! Perhaps going to my study, reading, lighting a candle and remembering others around the world and close by living with pain. It helps to have a fan heater available so I don't get cold in the night. Sometimes I listen to music through headphones on my pocket CD player ... calming, reassuring and beautiful music.

Medication

I have taken medication for pain for nearly twenty-five years; in the last year the strength of that medication has been increased. I am concerned about the slowness of my responses as a result, at times dullness. I was advised to speak first to the pharmacist, who in turn submitted a review to my GP. Is it possible to reduce the level of medication? Could this have beneficial effect without losing pain control?

My walking stick

I have inherited an old wooden walking stick and it has become a friend. It was handmade by Nils, Kerstin's father; he had polio as a child and limped throughout his adult life.

I use my walking stick not only to support and prop myself up but also to send out a message to people: 'Keep well clear of me, please.' On rare occasions I use crutches when out for a walk to reduce jarring in the spine, but they in turn increase pressure on my shoulders.

Breathing

When I am in pain I tense my body, and while this is the worst thing to do, it is also the most understandable. Somehow we must learn to relax, and yes, I know there are relaxation techniques, but when in pain common sense goes out of the window.

I have come late to the significance of breathing exercises. Vivien, as I have already explained elsewhere, began a small Prana group in Eileen and Barrie's lounge, and helped us into a way of deep, relaxing breathing which feels almost primal. Our every moment of breathing in and breathing out we take for granted; rarely do we pause within this mystery. Vivien draws from her experience as a yoga teacher. She has been wise and generous.

Depression

When I am in pain and I don't sleep, I get tired and often low. I have found it difficult to accept the notion of being depressed; perhaps we need help with this. I spoke of this during a visit to the Pain Management Clinic and it was suggested that I be referred to a psychologist, and I agreed. I heard nothing more and could have pursued it but didn't and wonder why.

'How are you?'

I am learning that we need to have a variety of replies to this daily question but all must contain some truth. We can help each other with this. Mostly I respond defiantly: 'I am well and I am in pain.' Or 'I am well and up and down.' At times I feel like saying: 'Do you really want to know?' And: 'How long have you got?!'

I am learning to be honest rather than heroic.

Baloo moments

I can only last around 45 minutes in my portable, collapsible chair and then pain can turn me to panic – it takes over, overriding memory and common sense. I know there is no need to wait until near breaking point before I stand up, stretch and walk around. I know that most people are more understanding and compassionate than I give them credit for, yet for some inexplicable reason I hang on through a resentful obstinacy and on occasions burst out in a way that shakes people, embarrasses Kerstin and leaves me feeling humiliated.

On sharing this with Merlin, he offered some unexpected advice. 'It's time you developed your own "Baloo moments". It is so important to live this level of frustration with strategies, which includes a lightness of touch and humour.' I didn't believe my ears. He reminded me of Baloo, the Disney bear in *The Jungle Book*: how periodically that loved bear stood on his hind legs and, while rubbing his back against a tree, sang his soul song, 'Bare Necessities'. Merlin continued: 'Buy yourself a Baloo and take it with you as a friend and mentor!' To Kerstin's embarrassment I bought myself a Baloo bear. 'You're not taking that bear to Sweden?!' she insisted. And I did.

Humour

I wonder about the importance of humour in the healing process. During one period in hospital my neighbour in the next bed was an old Irishman. He started telling stories before the early-morning trolley came around with tea. His stories took their place alongside the morning medication. 'My wife, God bless her, she packed my bag before I came into this place, and when I got here I discovered that she had packed two flannels … And what will I be doing with two flannels?' he asked. And her reply: 'Because you are a two-faced basket!'

From Archbishop Desmond Tutu I learned the interconnectedness of the struggle for social justice and laughter.

Gazing

I now have time to gaze, to listen and to wonder. Through our patio windows we look out into the garden and beyond to the massive trees of the skyline. The garden could be likened to an airport – tits, robins, sparrows, wrens, nuthatches, blackbirds, ringed doves and pigeons come to the feeders and peck up what falls to the ground. Our family response to the squirrels differs: they achieve unimaginable high-wire contortions on the feeders and leap across chasms from tree to tree; they also dig up bulbs in the winter and chew fresh buds in the springtime.

Large sinister-looking rooks sit on the highest branches of the conifers, swaying in the wind, surveying the terrain below. Small birds in the depths of the night sing *'while it is yet dark'*. Seagulls sit on a nearby rooftop with a well-measured spacing between them, while others swirl in circles and are suddenly seen swooping. Our back garden is an airport.

I water, sometimes over-water, the house plants throughout every season.

It is said of Donald Nicholl, highly respected author, academic and active worker for justice and peace, that in the last months of his life he gave up thinking and took up gazing.

Flying

A person who has come to see me for many years always brings with him a plastic bag from which he takes three things: his slippers, a gift and a diary into which he records the day and time of our next meeting. I have learned from him many things, including waiting through the long pauses. At the close of one period together, as he was passing my chair, he stopped, asking, 'And how are you, Donald?' My response surprised him and also myself. 'I am learning to fly,' was my spontaneous reply.

A few weeks later in the post I received an awesome photograph of two marsh harriers flying in harmony into billowing, storm-filled clouds. He understood.

I am encouraged by this piece by an unknown author. 'Ten things required for flying':

> '*A longing not to be grounded, an awareness of sky, time to imagine the delight of flying, energy to overcome inertia, belief that you can do it, a certain recklessness, courage to conquer fear of crashing, trust in invisible things, joyful abandon and a landing strip.*'

Chairs

And I almost forgot: chairs. After the second spinal operation in 1994, I was sent to the 'Ability Development Centre', and please note the significance of that name. The intention was to find a chair that would enable me to continue in my work. What was offered was a Norwegian Gravity Chair, and it has become a friend for life. It has four different positions, each taking the pressure off my spine. I now have three such chairs: one in Sweden, one in the study, provided by friends in Notting Hill, and one used in the dining and lounge areas of the house. The chair is large, not heavy but awkward for us to carry. The cushions are well-worn and from time to time the seat section loses its supportive resilience and needs renewing; however, the original manufacturer no longer makes the replacement parts.

I use another chair, lighter and more portable, when we go to church or visit friends. To date I have worn through about six of these. The quality of spinal support is limited, screws need tightening, and this has become a concern. As we grow older we increasingly need help carrying the chairs. Well-meaning, jovial onlookers pass irritating comments about the chairs and their occupant.

Richard Holloway, in the opening lines of his book *Doubts and Loves*, writes: '*Some years ago I copied into my notebook an aphorism from a Russian writer called V.V. Rozanov: "All religions will pass, but this will remain: simply sitting in a chair and looking in the distance."*'[1]

Note:

1. *Doubts and Loves: What Is Left of Christianity*, by Richard Holloway, Canongate, 2001, p.3

Praying the body, what could this look like?

'My body is much more than a mortal instrument of pleasure and pain. It is a home where God wants to manifest the fullness of the divine glory.' [1]

I recall the day when a kindly friend called from across the approach to the United College of the Ascension, 'How's your back nowadays, Donald?' My reply was mindless: I spoke of my body in a demeaning manner, as a remote 'it', as if my body and who I am are separate from each other. My intention was to be humorous, covering up the painful, frustrating reality.

There are friends who have led me into the foothills of what it means to pray through our body, the body that can radiate such health and well-being, bring such pleasure, and also be such a battlefield, experience such tormenting, withering pain.

I am learning that 'praying the body' includes an awareness of our human sexuality, our desire, our physical and emotional longing for intimacy, to hold and be held.

I am learning that 'praying the pain' includes starting with where we are: God is in our bodily pain.

I share what I am learning from my mentors and also discovering myself.

A body retreat

Bernie has lived with a serious spinal condition for many years; she conducts her work of spiritual direction while lying on her bed. I recall visiting her in hospital when she had a visitor, a sister from the same religious community. The sister was sitting quietly at the end of the bed massaging Bernie's feet. It was an act of cherishing. When the sister had gone Bernie grinned and said, 'Foot massage is wonderful. I can recommend it – and it also does wonders for bowels that are slow to move!'

Bernie tells of a 'body retreat' directed by a person who was both a La Retraite sister and also a physiotherapist. Over a period of eight days, through massage and conversation, Bernie was encouraged to reflect on the significance of different parts of her body within her own life story. She brought to mind and explored stories from the Bible, in particular stories in the New Testament that told of various parts of the human body. She permitted herself to be drawn into the mysterious interconnectedness of body, memory and unfolding story, and within this remembering conversed with God from the heart. Later she said, *'Every part of my body holds part of my story, a story with a past. Learn to listen and to learn from the story.'* And again: *'We live as resurrected people, with pain.'*

Praying the pain, the albatross prayer

The person who first introduced me to praying the pain was Michael Wilson, an elderly Anglican priest. Michael worked in the Pastoral Studies Department in Birmingham University, following a number of years on the staff of St Martin in the Fields, and had been for many years a doctor in Ghana. He was the nephew of Edward Wilson who went with Scott to the Antarctic where both men died. I accompanied Michael as his Eucharistic person during the last months of his life; he lived with a huge, fungating, cancerous tumour in his neck.

I recall a conversation with Michael in which we considered the place of pain in the Christian pilgrimage. Should it be zonked, anaesthetised? Michael asked about the validity of his sense of calling to meet pain not with morphine, but with an attempt to stand under it, a willingness to enter it, to learn what it is saying.

He spoke of his hope that pain entered into deeply can be transmuted into something for good on behalf of others. 'The mystery of the transmutation of pain cannot be explained or proved, only lived.' Michael's choice to decline medication for pain was a source of bewilderment and frustration to his family, his GP and the palliative care team at the hospice.

Michael's wish was that I should in time receive his books of explorations, musings and jottings. In them he wrote of the pain that returned in the night with a vengeance: '*a very angry, cold, tender lump, straining to grow at its inner end. Like hot burning rods, occasional knife thrusts, and at times the whole "rebellious lump" seemed to writhe with waves of pain as if a bag of worms ... then, after a few minutes' calm, it recurred again and again, from 2:00am until now 10:00am and it's still very sore and paining.*'

Michael searched for, and discovered, a framework for prayer within the living of his pain through the night hours; he called it his albatross plan. He loved the life of birds, their migration habits, their presence in his garden. Michael's notes were not as clear as I needed them to be. '*I constructed my albatross plan. The wandering albatross is programmed to fly a set route round the Antarctic (if male), or to the fishing grounds of South Africa (if female), then back to its nesting site. Yet it is also the freest of ocean-going birds to scent whatever opportunities of food and offal which come to it on the wind. So this plan is a skeleton of prayer, but free to wander.*'

It was arranged mnemonically (five fingers) so that he could follow it when distracted by pain:

1. *Silence. Opening myself to the love and prayers of so many people, 'I hold and am held', and 'I commit myself entire into your hands.'*

2. '*We relationships': our solidarity with those in pain, named family members and friends, ordered and not rambling.*

3. '*May this pain be of some use for someone, somewhere.'* (Michael believed that vicarious suffering is a matter of faith but 'immeasurable and controversial'.)

4. The albatross sets out into the night air following the scent, finding and touching the big ones: untreated Africans; victims of Hiroshima, Bhopal and Chernobyl; victims of earthquakes and hurricanes, and so on.

5. Thoughts for the night air and the albatross homing.

The 2:00am vigil: 'Offer it, toward God'

In the group 'Disabled and ministers', based in Birmingham, are people who are, or have been, in ministry, but for whom ministry has been affected or curtailed by a disability, depression or other illness. It includes nuns and priests, and one or two spouses also belong. Most have lived with physical limitation and pain for many years.

Jo was a member of the group. Highly intelligent and deeply Christian, she lived with severe cerebral palsy which left her with very little movement. She was unable to speak, so communicated by using a light attached to a sweatband on her head, which she pointed at a qwerty letter board to slowly spell out what she wanted to say. During our conversations, Jo attracted our attention by coughing, so that her light could be switched on.

At times Jo entered into a deep depression, sometimes for weeks or more. On one occasion the group talked together of 'the 2:00am vigil': that period of the dark night when we are at our lowest, most lonely, when our imaginations become twisted and distorted, when pain in the body and soul overwhelms, when the will to carry on and on diminishes. We shared our strategies for traversing these domains, until Jo made her familiar noises, wanting to contribute. She spelt out two words: 'Offer it.' And John, her husband, asked, 'Is that it? Can you say more?' Jo was silent. Then two more words: 'Toward God.' And Jo returned to silence with no further explanation. And this is what Jo taught us; this was her ministry to us.

She realigned our being before God: not asking God to remove us from our reality but rather offering our experience of body, of soul, our experience of chaos and disorder toward God. And this is the scary, wondrous mystery she has drawn us all into, and yes, we are right to be fearful, and also thankful, thankful to God.

I recall being invited to pray following that 2:00am vigil conversation and weaving into my words the hope that whatever was being offered toward God would be transformed. Later I felt ashamed, for that was not what Jo taught us: 'Offer it, toward God.' She was content to let God be God.

Jo died in March 2013.

Praying the body, my own discoveries

I was tired and in pain when I went to that Ash Wednesday service. My need was for quiet and for space for reflection for the liturgy of 'the ashing', for 'bread-breaking'. But on arrival in church I discovered that something quite different to my expectations was to be offered. Around the church, stalls were laid out and people were to be encouraged to visit each stall, pausing and pondering. Just when I was about to disappear down a plughole of resentful frustration we were offered an alternative: if we wished we could remain where we were, using the silence in any way that might be helpful for us.

I had forty minutes of silence in my chair. It was what I most needed.

To pray the body, what could that mean? …

To pay attention to the pain in my neck, shoulders, upper and lower back and in my legs, to listen for what is being communicated to me.

To ponder the Passion of Jesus from the perspective of what his body bore within that journey.

His utter exhaustion through the night trials, the stripping, the flogging with bone-studded thongs, the cross of thorns, the carrying and stumbling and falling under the weight of the cross, the help offered by Simon of Cyrene, the stretching out naked on the cross, the offer of drugged wine, the nailing of the hands, the feet smashed, the side pierced with a spear. His enduring of the pain, the cry of dereliction, the women watching, the soldiers and others drinking and jeering …

Then there was a 'coming into mind' of people whom I know and love, people who live with pain, 'the pain-bearers': Bernie, Steve, Kjell, Sally, Peter, Ron, Joyce, Sue, Ille and so many others.

From this naming and holding emerged a mysterious awareness of the showing of the hands of Jesus, his touching blind eyes, deaf ears, dumb mouths, his lifting of the condemned woman cast down in the dust, his arms open to embrace the leper, his hands gently yet firmly washing the feet of his friends, the marks of the nails in his hands, the sense of the blessings of those hands.

Then we were called out of our silence and into an awareness of each other and into a brief concluding ritual.

An inner homecoming

I have lived a bumpy transition into an unwelcome reality, yet within it discovered the paradox of an inner homecoming. *'Go to your cell and your cell will teach you.'*

During the busy travelling years I lived with the questions: Do we have to go away to a monastery to discover what we find in the monastery? Do we have to go away in order to come to the inner home, the inner cave, our own inner necessary place?

I am slowly learning the wondrous ways of the human body and more: God has made our body, with its capacity for great pleasure and acute pain, God's dwelling place and home, and more – through the journey into the depths of our humanity we may meet God.

The journey into the inner hermitage or the heart room is not an escape, on the contrary it is a journey into the heart of the world. Bishop John Austin spoke of prayer as *'standing in the heart room utterly unprotected'*. This is the context of attentiveness, of listening with the ear of the heart.

> *'When you are sad, tired, lonely and full of suffering, take refuge in the sanctuary of your soul, and there you will find your brother, your friend Jesus, who will console you, support you and strengthen you.'* [2]

And in conclusion, two prayers:

> *Jesus, my body has brought such pleasure and such pain; help me to listen with care and to attend with respect.*

> *May the wounds we carry become signs of resurrection?* [3]

Notes:

1. From *The Road to Daybreak: A Spiritual Journey*, Henri Nouwen, p.201, Darton, Longman & Todd, London, 2013. Used by permission of the publishers

2. Charles de Foucauld in his *Meditations of a Hermit*, source unknown

3. Bishop John Austin, source unknown

Ageing, 'Yes' to the next stage of the journey: the consent to be transformed

A letter to a friend, January 2011

In a recent letter you asked how I am and my response was to say that I am in 'a turning time', also I have not yet found words for this next stage of the journey. So often in my correspondence I sidestep the question and offer the lame phrase 'more later'.

At one level I recognise paradox within myself, a slow realignment – a desire to withdraw yet also to engage with life in a deeper way, a longing for silence yet an inner busyness which colludes with avoidance, an inner emptiness which also holds a sense of necessity and anticipation, an enjoyment of one-to-one relationships and also a deepening sense of communion, an interrelatedness with the absent ones. We live within the thin line, the veil, the membrane twixt earth and heaven, and within the foretaste of what it is to belong to the worshipping community, both here and beyond. We move already into worship, worship with the communion of saints. I wonder more and more about the story of Jesus' transfiguration.

There is an awareness of living into 'the last furlong', an increasing sense of the laying down, the letting go, a letting go which includes sadness but is not morbid; not resignation nor rejection but rather a freedom to be gathered into the waiting future, a surrender into an emerging. A friend speaks of *'a moving from all who I am toward what I have not yet become'*.

Within the incompleteness, flawedness, messiness, fragility, forgetfulness, contraction, stripping, there is an inner yielding toward something more profound, a 'yes' to the next stage of the journey, a consenting, a desire to be still growing within it all, more alive within the present moment, a being drawn more deeply into the life of the God who waits for us.

There are hints of deeper dimensions of a greater wholeness. *'Wholeness includes regrets, and regrets are so different from the sterile "if onlys".'* [1]

Within this complexity, a return to simplicity and playfulness and joy and gazing.

Within the fears, there is a freedom, a trusting, no longer being a prisoner of fear.

I am reminded that all this belongs to *'the consent to be transformed'*,[2] the yielding and entrusting into the unimaginable beyond. It is within this mystery I have few words or images.

Notes:

1. From a letter from Jean Head. Jean is a wise old friend, whom I first grew to know well in Notting Hill.

2. Thomas Keating. See *Consenting to God as God Is*

An 'Aha moment'

Jottings in my journal

Early one morning around 3:00am, I was in my room and in pain, and in the silence attempting as best I could to hold before God people who are in my heart: in my imagination attempting to kneel with them before the cross. I am physically not good at kneeling.

Then a scene emerged from deep down – so alive, vivid and vibrant. It was of Jesus 'already there', kneeling at the feet of those who are in my heart, those I attempt to hold before God. He was gentle and kind, talking and laughing, washing feet, massaging aching shoulders, rubbing sore backs and wiping the arse for those who can no longer do it for themselves, like dear Michael, a friend with motor neuron disease. Jesus turned and looked at me over his shoulder as he continued his gentle and loving work. He smiled with such mischievous warmth and said, 'Donald, I beat you to it. I am here already!'

And it was then, and remains, an 'Aha moment'!

I attempt to hold so much, so many in my heart, and feel I offer so little, only the holding. Then I discover the One who is already here/there ... gentle, loving and at work mostly hidden, unrecognised.

There is also something in all this about the human body, the sacredness of our body, at times with cancer, MND, MS, spines aching, people with dementia, people with broken hearts, at times living with utter powerlessness and exhaustion. It is the bodiliness of his gentle yet firm attention that moves me so deeply. And I hear my own whisper: 'Not only my feet but my head as well.'

I wonder what all this means.

And more: when I was convalescing a few years ago, a friend sent me a card with a candle on it and these words: *'When the candle is lit angels gather.'* And also: *'And angels come in many forms.'* I've never been one for angels, and the person who sent the card isn't either, so I was surprised and it made me wonder.

I would describe the man who treats my spine each week as one belonging to the 'foot washers'. He would be embarrassed to be called an angel. But isn't that what he is, an angel, a 'bringer of blessing'?

Transforming encounters

There are three encounters I want to share, each very different, all transformative in ways I could not have anticipated. They have drawn me into a fresh awareness of what it is to kneel, hearken and see through to the heart of things.

The arrival of asylum seekers in a small Swedish village: discovering the human being in each other

Selma Lagerlöf's Swedish novel *Jerusalem* (for which she became the first woman to be awarded the Nobel Prize for Literature) was written in 1901. The book is based on the true story of the emigration of 37 men, women and children, who, on 23rd July, 1896, left their farms and families in the parish of Nås in the province of Dalarna, Sweden. They travelled by horse and carriage, by train, by ship, crossing the Mediterranean via Malta to Jaffa in Palestine. Their destination was Jerusalem; their intention was to join the American colony there, and to wait, wait for Jesus to come. Selma Lagerlöf visited them in Jerusalem in 1900.

Over a century later, on the 23rd of July, 2011, the same number of men, women and children (37 people, 9 families) arrived in Nås: asylum seekers designated by the immigration authority to wait, wait in this vast area of silent forests and lakes, wait to learn if they were to be granted permission to remain in Sweden. Most of the asylum seekers had left large urban areas, some had travelled for months across land and sea, all of them were exhausted. They were provided with temporary accommodation in 'Legoland', vacant flats built in 1986. Close by their new homes is the Västerdalälven, the deep, wide, slowly moving river that once carried logs to the saw mills.

There is a bridge across that river and the road leads not only to the pizzeria and the shop in the Gulf petrol station, but also to a church in Nås (Missionhuset). The small congregation is known to be an open, welcoming and hospitable community. Some are former members of the Baptist Church and others of the Swedish Mission Covenant Church, both being drawn into a wider ecumenical pilgrimage known as Equmeniakyrkan. They have no ordained pastor, there is no resident priest in the parish church and, at the time of writing, it has only a handful of regular worshippers.

Among them is Siv Hansson, who has a Baptist background and a licence to preach in the Church of Sweden. In the summer of 2011 she retired and 'waited on God' to guide her into some new task. It was while attending a village meeting that Siv first learned of the needs of the asylum seekers: winter and summer clothing, boots and shoes, toys, prams, bicycles and also a place to store and distribute what was being given by the local people. The asylum seekers also needed a place to meet. Siv says she is 'normally cautious', however on this occasion her overwhelming impulse was to be spontaneous: 'We have our church!'

The next morning, at a meeting for prayer, Siv shared the information and her plans.

In the afternoon she prepared an invitation to *fika* (coffee and cakes) then immediately went to the flats occupied by the asylum seekers, found some of the women talking, and handed them the invitation; somehow she communicated the warmth of genuine welcome.

So it was that on Wednesday 27th July, 2011, while her friend Berit prepared the coffee, buns and cookies (*bullar och kakor*), that Siv went to 'Legoland', met the families and led them over the bridge to the open door of welcome. This was certainly not on the list Siv offered to God for her new life.

Every Wednesday since that day, in summer and winter, asylum seekers have crossed the bridge in Nås, pushing prams, cycling, walking on their way to what has become known as Öppet Hus, the 'Open House for All'. These families come from Afghanistan, Iraq, the Ukraine, Syria, Somalia, Nigeria, Albania, Azerbaijan … They have arrived in a place of waiting. And in the months that have followed some have been returned to their country of origin, or country of first entry into Europe; others have been granted permits to remain and to make Sweden their new home. Through all the pain and relief of both the leaving and arriving, the warmth of hospitality in the 'Open House for All' is offered. Of course it is not easy to understand each other through all the different languages, yet both asylum seekers and volunteers are discovering the human being in each other.

The story of the 'Open House for All' continues to unfold. The asylum seekers bring letters and forms from schools, from doctors and lawyers, from the immigration authority and ask for help to fill them in. Much of this work is done by Pej, a retired farmer and former Chairman of the Parish Council, who patiently and with skill uses his laptop to process translations. Sometimes he visits people in their flats. On occasion volunteers take asylum seekers to appointments by car. One day a woman with diabetes, who was also pregnant, was taken with her husband and children to the hospital in Mora. On the way home the thankful father, a Muslim, asked to be brought first to the chapel to pray.

Both the children and parents need to learn Swedish. The children, who are pupils in local schools, receive extra help during vacations – and learn quickly. During term time their parents are offered informal Swedish language classes staffed by retired teachers. Some of the families need help with money. A special fund has been created, and a donation to that fund comes from 'Erikshjälpen', a large and busy second-hand store in the neighbouring village, Dala-Järna. This is a Christian charity and the manager is a Palestinian refugee. Some of the asylum seekers work in Erikshjälpen as volunteers. There is also now football in the village sports hall for the children and their fathers. Siv's husband is the proud trainer of the 'Nås Global Football Team'.

On July 29th, 2015 we marked four years of hospitality at Öppet Hus. 'We have met people of other faiths and cultures,' Siv said. 'We are learning to accept each other; we like each other. Nobody leaves their home and work without a good reason. For us life has become meaningful.'

The team of volunteers has grown. The goodwill and generosity in the wider community increases. The asylum seekers enjoy *fika*, the men still sit together, sharing their stories, the women still sit around the edge. All still wait, wait for news. And the children still play, sing, dance, eat *'bullar och kakor'* and drink their fruit juice.

And Siv's prayer? The prayer is full of thankfulness for the way God continues to provide. She also asks that God will send a pastor to help them worship in their new situation.

Friday evening hospitality

In the autumn of 2015 Siv sent us a message saying that a further one hundred asylum seekers were scheduled to arrive the following day and to take up residence in the old hospital. Already the team at Öppet Hus was gathering winter clothes and making plans to extend Wednesday hospitality to Friday evenings also. There have been periods when almost two hundred asylum seekers have lived their waiting in the village. On occasions up to a hundred asylum seekers have made their way through the freezing winter to the warmth of the Friday evening hospitality at Öppet Hus.

Continuing to discover the human being in each other

In July 2016 there was a party to celebrate five years of Öppet Hus – and the chapel was full. The representative from the *kommun*, the local authority, expressed thanks and encouragement, bringing with her three very large *tårtor* (gateaux covered with marzipan and filled with cream).

The team of volunteers has grown to twenty. While the goodwill and generosity in the wider community increases, there can also be opposition. Of course it is still not easy to understand each other through the different languages, yet both asylum seekers and village volunteers are continuing to discover the human being in each other.

During the summer of 2016 Kerstin and I were invited to lead a service of worship for the small number of Christian and English-speaking asylum seekers. They were joined by Öppet Hus volunteers and people from churches in neighbouring villages. A Ukrainian woman sang, a Syrian woman read Psalm 23, Siv paraphrased the story of Hagar (Gen 16, 21:1–21), and was clearly deeply touched.

I began to preach, exploring the meaning of the Hagar story for us, when the doors of the chapel opened – and in poured over thirty asylum seekers with their families, most of them Muslims, 'the children of Hagar'. We put the service on pause and welcomed 'the new members of the family'. Without being told, the children made their way into the back room where they normally meet to have their drinks and cakes, paint and draw. The adults were found seats. It was an overwhelming sight; the village chapel was almost full – imagine what our village forebears would have thought to see such a scene! We lit candles and prayed for each of the countries represented. After singing a hymn we gathered around tables for *fika*. The children of the asylum seekers helped their parents and grandparents into conversations. One veiled woman from Afghanistan told how members of her family had been beheaded by the Taliban; she grieved for the victims of the bombs in Kabul the previous day. The twelve-year-old son of a man from Mongolia helped his father to ask his questions.

On returning to Birmingham we wrote to Siv telling her how inspired we were by the sustained work of warm, wise hospitality in Öppet Hus. We responded to her question concerning worship in their new situation, adding further biblical stories belonging to our shared faith heritage. We asked if they could imagine the village church becoming not only Öppet Hus but also a place of silence for Muslims and Christians, and those whose faith is known to God alone: a place of silent prayer where candles could be lit, where grief, fear, outrage, painful memories, and also gratitude and hope, could all be acknowledged before the One God.

We have promised Siv, her colleagues and members of their new family, the children of Hagar, our continued prayers.

Where East meets West: Istanbul

This short visit to Istanbul was made possible by our daughter Nicola and her husband, Ben, who have lived in Turkey since 2014.

The writing began as necessary jottings in my journal.

I was unprepared for the encounter in Istanbul.

'We'll eat a fish sandwich,' our daughter said as we approached the quayside in old Istanbul. Ashore with our cases and my portable chair we were soon engulfed into a great multitude; boys whom we'd never met before hurriedly found space and a place for the chair, without any hint of lingering for money. It was a kind of picnic – a feeding of the 5000. Everywhere queues at stalls, smoke rising from grills, people sitting and standing in groups, young women, young men, old women, old men, everyone eating bread and fish – freshly grilled mackerel with fried onions.

Our hotel was close by Aya Sofya, known also as Hagia Sophia, and the Sultan Ahmed Mosque, more widely known as the Blue Mosque, their minarets and domes rising in awesome dignity, lit up at sunset.

Our restaurant was also close by, in an open sunken market, with men, and women also, sitting around puffing their long pipes, white smoke first billowing then drifting, and on their knees balanced iPhones. There was exotic food and wine, live music and a whirling white dervish, whirling into mystic realms. The streets were full and festive, shops and eating places were wide open, bright and beckoning.

In contrast people who had arrived from Syria slumped in small human piles on the pavements, coats wrapped around against the chill night air, empty plastic boxes waiting for any loose cash: a waiting mother and her two children under five years old; a child on her own, perhaps three or four years of age; a thin, sad lone boy holding a piece of paper: 'I am from Syria.'

The following day we bought tickets to enter Aya Sofya, the church which through the centuries became a mosque then a museum. I learned that Hagia Sophia was rebuilt in her present form between 532 and 537 under the personal supervision of Emperor Justinian I, and that on several occasions the structures had been severely damaged by earthquakes. For over 900 years this magnificently repaired building was the seat of the Orthodox Patriarch of Constantinople and a principal setting for Church councils and imperial ceremonies. During our visit to Turkey we heard rumours that the recently re-elected President of Turkey, Recep Tayyip Erdoğan, intends to transform the museum back into a mosque.

It was under the dome of Aya Sofya that my chair was placed and where I sat alone for an hour, alone, yet not alone, tourists with guides, headphones and cameras all gazing into this masterpiece of Byzantine architecture, at the golden mosaics of Virgin and Child, of Christ and Emperor Constantine. From under centuries of thick yellow-painted plaster Byzantine paintings have been discovered. High up on the great pillars hang Islamic roundels.

I sat alone, and yet not alone, listening for what can still be heard within all this history, a drifting mantra within me coming and going, rising and falling: '*Thou, O Lord, art in our midst.*'

Meanwhile some more tourists, smiling and murmuring among themselves at the sight of the old man in the chair, asked if it was OK to take my photograph.

Outside – and into the sunshine and the great welcoming spaces the call to prayer blasted out through loudspeakers antiphonally, almost playfully alternating, from the Blue Mosque to the smaller mosque close by Aya Sofya:

Allahu Akbar (God is Great) said four times ...

Ashhadu an la ilaha illa Allah (I bear witness that there is no god except the One God) said twice …

There are two entrances to the Blue Mosque; one queue is for those who come to pray and the other for visitors. My chair was placed in the large forecourt among those mingling and quietly queuing to enter for prayer. I sat alone for an hour in the sun, alone, and yet not alone, among young and old, women, men and children – Muslims from every corner of the world. 'Salam': a huge African beamed down his blessing on me. Here no tickets were needed; we took off our shoes, placed them in a plastic bag and carried them.

The imperial mosque was built on the site of the palace of Byzantine emperors following Turkey's crushing defeat in the war with Persia (1603-1618). A defiant and proud act in the face of humiliation, and it was the poor who suffered most through increased deprivation.

My portable chair was placed near the prayer area under the main dome. I gazed up at the twenty thousand handmade ceramic tiles with their over fifty traditional designs … at the great chandeliers where it is said ostrich eggs can be found, their smell reputed to repel spiders … at the two hundred intricate stained-glass windows … and at the great tablets on the walls inscribed with verses from the Quran and the names of caliphs … Around the circumference of the mosque were private enclosures for women withdrawn out of sight for prayer, while under the dome, men prostrated themselves in full view on lush carpets.

I sat alone, and yet not alone, listening for what can still be heard within all this history, a drifting mantra coming and going, rising and falling: '*Thou, O Lord, art in our midst.*'

During his trip to Turkey in November 2006, Pope Benedict XVI visited the Blue Mosque: only the second time in history a Pope has visited a Muslim place of worship.

After taking off his shoes, the Pope paused for a moment of silent meditation with the Mufti of Istanbul and the Imam of the Blue Mosque.

Then the Pope *'thanked divine Providence for this ... May all believers identify themselves with the one God and bear witness to true brotherhood.'* He said that Turkey *'will be a bridge of friendship and collaboration between East and West'.* Then he thanked the people of Turkey for their *'cordiality and sympathy'* during his trip; he said he *'felt loved and understood'.* [1]

We returned to Birmingham; and on the next day I joined the men in our local mosque in the next street. With them I took off my shoes. There was a kindness and thoughtfulness in their welcome. Without hesitation one of the men found a chair and led me to a convenient place near the front of the large carpeted prayer room. Already there were five long lines of men kneeling, squatting and prostrating themselves. There were no women present. It is now two days since the shootings in Paris. Our prayer is to the Creator, the All-Merciful, it is for all humanity and it is for ourselves.

I am alone, yet not alone.

Within the coming and going, the rising and falling, the drifting mantra remains: *'Thou, O Lord, art in our midst.'*

Note:

1.   Reported on a number of websites

The return of Godflesh: barking back

Morning-after reflections following an extraordinary Saturday night – a first visit to the Supersonic Festival.

Could this also be a glimpse of transformation?

I've grown to love our son-in-law Ben, but not understand the supersonic world of music that has partially shaped him. He was brought up on the Beatles and the Beach Boys, and so I wonder what drew Ben into hard rock, into *'the world of extreme music'*, apocalyptic sounds and images *'steeped in a Birmingham setting'*.

His music emerged at the end of the Thatcher years as a protest from working-class east Birmingham youth: *'a barking back'*, *'an act of cleansing and purifying'* from so much that poisoned the air, dehumanised political and social systems, holding the people down.

I have grown to know something of the Ben who, after years of touring the world with the influential band Godflesh, chose to withdraw from everything associated with the almost deafening noise, into a whole year alone, hidden away in the silent folds of the Cambrian Mountains in Wales, a small and simple cottage his solitary home. This Ben I begin to know. What I can't understand is how Ben and other gentle, sensitive, thoughtful men, and no doubt women also, are drawn into supersonic hard rock music. All this exploding noise, and within it these gentle human beings.

And last night?

Late last night we went to 'the Custard Factory' under the railway arches near the bus station in the centre of Birmingham. Why? It was an opportunity to enter Ben's world and to attempt to understand more.

It was freezing cold when we passed through the entrance gate for performers' guests – walking into the open-air corridors lit up by strong spotlights, watched by large, vigilant, yellow-vested security men, past halls already pulsating with music – and on into a building resembling a large empty aircraft hangar. No heating, no chairs, only a cold concrete floor.

Godflesh was headlining the festival. And men, lots and lots of them, young men between 35-45 years of age, wrapped up warm, some with woolly hats, flooded in just before the band took to the stage, men filling the hall, waiting. And when the crashing interlude music faded, Ben and Justin appeared amidst rising, swelling cheers, and then an explosion – swirling red, yellow, green and white lights, a rhythmic bludgeoning, a primal pounding within an almost overwhelming sound and billowing white clouds enveloping the stage and hanging over us, like incense filling a temple. And then the waves of chanting, the lifting up of hands and arms, the punching of the air, the gentle slow movement of heads, the swaying of bodies.

Godflesh travelled the world until the late 1990s and this was their homecoming, their first concert in Birmingham since 1991. The reuniting fans, including some who had travelled from other countries just for the show, sang – sang along with the songs as if they had never left their hearts. And the chanting? 'G.C. Green' – the rhythmic repeating of our Ben's name.

And the paradox?

Such an erupting explosion of noise, such tortured images, including a yellow cross, flashed across the blue screens, and the gentle swaying, relaxed movement of young men and a few young women. The experience was much more than I had expected. I hesitate to articulate my wonderings: Is there, somewhere within all this, a public ritual, an exorcising of what some experience as their demons? *'An act of cleansing and purifying'*?

And then the lights went up, the volume of the noise went down and people hung around, well-pleased. A group of them, recognising my age and culture, asked if I had enjoyed it. My explanation for being there was that I had followed Ben to the festival to try to understand the world he had once inhabited. 'Tell him, he's a mean bass. Tell him – congratulations.'

From the Supersonic Festival programme:

'It's quite a year for Supersonic. Swans and Godflesh, two of the most influential bands in the world of extreme music, headlining the festival. While Swans took inspiration from their New York backdrop, across the pond Godflesh's sound was steeped in its Birmingham setting. Justin Broadrick claimed he wanted to create the sound of the "scum" that surrounded him. Drawing as much from acts like Throbbing Gristle and Whitehouse as Black Sabbath, they created industrial metal, an apocalyptic noise of the starkest kind. Supersonic is proud to host the original line-up performing a homecoming show.'

Epilogue

Another 'Aha moment'

'Unite us with him for ever
and bring us with the whole creation
to your eternal kingdom.' [1]

From jottings in my journal

I was so tired and in such pain, just kind of 'hanging on in there', when something happened and I am almost embarrassed to write it down. I have scarcely shared it with anyone but do so now from those almost unreadable jottings. I am not given to having visions but this could be likened to one.

It was so alive, vivid. I was being drawn into much more than a glancing passing scene: it felt primal, all-pervading, inner, yet so widely communal – a deep flowing within continuity, drawn into an essential interconnectedness, the we-ness within past and future and present, drawn toward and into the 'heart', a pulsating, throbbing heart, in company with those who have gone before.

There was such a sense of well-being, of *'all will be well'*, and *'well'* within such a liberating inclusiveness, a communion I have heard spoken of, even glimpsed, yet this was something even more all-embracing: all creation, all humanity, all time, both within and beyond all time.

For a moment which I did not want to end, I was, am, will be as one alive within the hidden pulse, the flow, within this subter-ranean communion.

And that's it, that's it.

And the music, but where's the eternal music?

And then I became aware of where I was and the quiet, beckoning invitation to join the slowly moving queues, then the huge heaving out of my uncomfortable chair aided by Pappa Nils' 100-year-old walking stick, and the leaning into Kerstin's holding arm and moving towards 'the kneeling', all with open hands for the broken bread and the scarcely heard murmurings, *'The body of Christ, the blood of Christ, keep you in eternal life. Amen'* ...

Note:

1. *Methodist Worship Book*, from 'Holy Communion for the Ordinary Season' (first order), p.194, Methodist Publishing

A letter

Human Anatomy Unit,
Institute of Clinical Sciences,
University of Birmingham

Dear Professor,

Thank you for your letter.

… My donation arises from a sense of gratitude. The imagery of 'handing over and entrusting' is significant for me. I am an adopted person, 'handed over' into a nursery hotel within the first few hours of my life; three months later I was 'entrusted' to my new parents. My adopted brother and I have been very fortunate: we were loved equally and differently. In addition, over the last 25 years I have received the skill and experience of the NHS through a series of major surgical operations, so 'handing over and entrusting' is woven into my story.

I am a Methodist minister and for me the 'handing over and entrusting of my body' belongs to my understanding of the Eucharist. It is both a symbol of my thanksgiving and also the hope that the handing over of my body can somehow enrich the common good.

Which leads me to a question. Are you aware of others who have searched for a ritual, a liturgy to be used prior to death as a means of expressing sacramental thankfulness? [1]

When I have received further information from you I will make sure that my wife and two daughters have a copy among their relevant papers.

Yours sincerely,
Donald Eadie (Revd)

Note:

1. My search for an existing liturgy/ritual/prayer that could be used in the handing over of my body for research yielded almost nothing. The guidance was: 'Donald, write your own.' This I have done, drawing from a beautiful and insightful draft written by two friends.

A prayer for handing over and entrusting

God, you offer your very self through everything,
the membranes of our lives,
the intermingling of joy and sorrow,
surprising, unfolding, enfolding.
'In the heights and in the depths be praise.' [1]

God, you sustain us through wilderness times, Gethsemane times.
You strengthen us through angels,
angels in so many forms.
'In the heights and in the depths be praise.'

God, you mark our body with the sign of the cross,
children of the Way of Jesus.
You party with us.
You hold us in our pain-bearing.
You draw us into a future we could not have imagined.
'In the heights and in the depths be praise.'

God, help us with our letting go,
our handing over, our entrusting,
our yielding into the flow,
divine life within all life.
'In the heights and in the depths be praise.'

God, you draw us into the bumpy road
that leads into your deep love.
You draw us into your heart,
your silence, your compassion.
'In the heights and in the depths be praise.'

Donald Eadie

Note:

1. Walter Chalmers Smith (1824-1908)

A Eucharistic liturgy
and other resources

A Eucharistic liturgy

This liturgy emerged from the conferences hosted at Sarum College in which we explored 'the faith journey of impaired pilgrims'.[1]

Opening:

Thou, O Lord, art in our midst:
Life-giver, Truth-revealer, Compassionate One.

'If the Spirit is the source of our life, let the Spirit also direct our course.' (Galatians 5:25)

Mysterious Spirit of God,
You are known through our unknowing:
you are the wind that lifts the wing,
and the Wild Goose that flies upon it.
You are the light within the darkness,
and the darkness itself.
You are the Discomforting Comforter, bringing us peace,
yet shaking our comfortable lives.
And we meet you in the man Jesus,
who welcomed those who were an uncomfortable presence,
listened to their stories
and placed their reality
at the heart of his ministry.

Mysterious Spirit of God,
you still sweep over the face of the waters,
still groan within all creation,
still move within all humanity.
Receive our worship.

Confession:

In the community of Christ's church and in the presence of God's people, I confess to God that I have sinned in thought, word and deed. I have not loved God, cared for God's world or respected God's people as I should. I own my responsibility and pray for God's pardon.

May God forgive you, Christ befriend you and the Spirit renew and change your life. Amen

In the community of Christ's church and in the presence of God's people, I confess to God that I have sinned in thought, word and deed. I have not loved God, cared for God's world or respected God's people as I should. I own my responsibility and pray for God's pardon.

May God forgive you, Christ befriend you and the Spirit renew and change your life. Amen

Scripture reading

Prayers of intercession:

Spirit of God, we give thanks
that you are met and known
through the breaking and outpouring
of the life of Jesus.
Meet us now in those
regarded as an uncomfortable presence,
whose lives share in his brokenness.
Open us to meet you through them.

Through those who cannot see,
help us to embrace darkness.

Through those whose movement is restricted,
help us to embrace stillness.

Through those whose remembering is fragile,
help us to embrace the present.

Through those who cannot hear,
help us to embrace silence.

Through those dependent upon others,
and those who care for others,
help us to embrace our connection.

Through all those rejected as 'different'
help us to embrace our unity
in which diversity is celebrated
as your empowering gift to us ...

Through fire and water
you have brought us.

Through storm and bitter hurt
you have brought us.

Through searing pain and bitter wound
you have brought us.

Through years of searching and of longing
you have brought us.

Day after day, night after night.
To this time and place.

With friends and companions
you have brought us

With searching, discovery and delight
you have brought us.

With pilgrims of age and the laughter of childhood
you have brought us.

With pilgrims of many faiths and of none
you have brought us.

Surrounded by and one with all the saints in light
you have brought us.

Day after day, night after night.
To this time and place.

The Lord's Prayer (each person is encouraged to pray in their own mother tongue)

The Peace:

Christ, who nourishes us, is our peace. Strangers and friends, male and female, old and young, he has broken down the barriers we erect, to bind us to him and to each other. Let us share his peace.

The Peace of the Lord be always with you.
And also with you.

The Peace is shared.

Offertory prayer:

Lord and Giver of every good thing,
we bring you
bread and wine for our communion,
lives and gifts for your kingdom,
all for transformation through your grace and love,
made known in Jesus Christ our Lord.
Amen

The thanksgiving:

God of mystery,
known through the crucified,
whose power refashions weakness and strength,
whose presence is embodied through brokenness,
we offer our awe and wonder.
With those who are broken by pain,
with those exhausted by the struggle to conform,
with those crippled by the insensitivity of others,
with those not seen as a resource but only as a concern,
we praise you, saying,
Holy, holy, holy
God of vulnerable love.
Heaven and earth proclaim your glory.
Hosanna in the highest.
Blessed is he who reveals
the reality of God.

We bless the name of Jesus,
bone of our bone,
flesh of our flesh,
whose brokenness and suffering make love real,
who on the night in which he was betrayed
took bread, gave thanks, broke it
and gave it to his disciples, saying,
'Take, eat. This is my body which is for you.
Do this in remembrance of me.'

After supper he took the cup, saying,
'Drink from this, all of you; this is my blood given for you.
Do this whenever you drink it in remembrance of me.'

Christ has died,
Christ is risen,
Christ redeems our stories.

As we eat this bread and drink this cup
we acknowledge brokenness as a path to truth.
We long for the bread of tomorrow:
eternally broken and so able to nourish.
We long for the new wine of the kingdom:
continuously poured out that thirst may be quenched.

Spirit of wisdom, brood over these bodily things
and make us one body with Christ
so that in the life of a changing world
the broken may lead us towards wholeness,
the suffering show us the way to peace
and the excluded teach us of community,
so that all may receive
the gifts to be found
within the body of Christ.
Amen[2]

The breaking of the bread:

May this bread, and its breaking be blessed.
May the broken peoples of the world be blessed.
May we, in our wholeness and brokenness,
be blessed and so become signs of resurrection.
Amen

Jesus, Lamb of God,
have mercy on us.

Jesus, bearer of our sins,
have mercy on us.

Jesus, redeemer of the world,
grant us peace.

Invitation to the table:

These are the gifts of God to nourish us in our living of the Way of Jesus.

Draw near in faith and thanksgiving.

The sharing of the bread and wine

Prayer:

Mysterious Spirit of God,
**we rejoice in thanksgiving
that you meet us in our vulnerability.**

**That you walk beside us,
taking our pace and heeding our story.**

**That you turn the tables on us,
guest becoming host and feeding us,
giving us a taste of the flavour of the banquet
set for all people,
so we follow you out into the world
to live to your glory.
Amen**

The blessing:

God, in your mercy,
transform your groaning creation.

Christ, in your mercy,
transform our broken humanity.

Spirit, in your mercy,
transform our dispirited Church.

Father, Son and Holy Spirit,
draw us, like the bread,
into the mystery of transformation.

And the blessing of God,
Creator, Redeemer and Life-giver,
be among us and upon the many peoples of the earth.
Amen

Notes:

1. The liturgy draws on extracts from Peter Cole's 'Pentecost Eucharistic Prayer' and the 'Eucharistic Prayer' written for the 'Faith Journey of Impaired Pilgrims' conference at Sarum College, 2006 © Peter J. Cole. The liturgy also draws on prayers by Inderjit Bhogal, Bill Denning and Donald Eadie. Material used with permission.

2. Liturgical tradition includes a short prayer, the epiclesis, prior to the breaking of the bread petitioning the Holy Spirit to 'come down' on the elements, 'that these gifts of bread and wine may be for us the body and blood of Christ'. The Eucharistic liturgy developed from the Sarum conferences prays, 'Spirit of wisdom, brood over these bodily things and make us one body with Christ.'

    A helpful and gracious correspondence has emerged exploring the theological differences. An alternative prayer is offered:

    Come, Spirit of Holy Wisdom,
    breath birthing at creation,
    dying breath of the Saviour,
    that these gifts of bread and wine
    may be for us the body and blood of Christ,
    broken for our brokenness,
    poured out for our wholeness. Amen

Other resources

Bless the brokenness of the world (An intercessory prayer)

Holy God
as we break and hold this bread
we hold and offer to you:

The brokenness of those who live and struggle
with hunger and disease,
the brokenness of those who are excluded,
the brokenness of communities and neighbourhoods,
the brokenness in relationships between nations,
the brokenness in household and personal relationships,
the brokenness in relationships between different faiths,
the brokenness in relationships between Christian denominations,
the brokenness within congregations,
the brokenness we carry within our own bodies,
the brokenness we know when death tears away our loved ones.

As we hold and offer you this broken bread,
and as we eat it,
help us to keep trusting you are there
in the midst of all our brokenness.

Bless the brokenness of the world
and the broken people of the world.
Bless them and bless us.
Make us signs of resurrection.
Strengthen us to share in your work.
Feed us now and evermore,
and feed the world so that none may be hungry
and all may know welcome and hospitality.
In the name of Christ.
Amen [1]

Inderjit Bhogal

Transform our lives through grace and love (An offertory prayer)

Prepared through the Pain and Hope Group, PH7, for use in the Service of Prayer for Healing and Wholeness, Methodist Worship Book.

God, your Spirit breathes through all creation.
You have made our bodies your dwelling place and home.
You offer yourself through everything.
Transform our lives through grace and love.

We bring to you
bread and wine for our communion.
Lives and gifts for your kingdom.
You offer yourself through everything.
Transform our lives through grace and love.

We bring the miracle that is our human body, our joy, our pain.
You offer yourself through everything.
Transform our lives through grace and love.

We bring our vulnerability.
You offer yourself through everything.
Transform our lives through grace and love.

We bring our forgetfulness.
You offer yourself through everything.
Transform our lives through grace and love.

We bring our wounds, our scars.
You offer yourself through everything.
Transform our lives through grace and love.

We bring our aloneness.
You offer yourself through everything.
Transform our lives through grace and love.

We bring our depression.

You offer yourself through everything.
Transform our lives through grace and love.

We bring our disease, our unease.
You offer yourself through everything.
Transform our lives through grace and love.

We bring our anger.
You offer yourself through everything.
Transform our lives through grace and love.

We bring our tears.
You offer yourself through everything.
Transform our lives through grace and love.

We bring our 'yes' to transformation,
our openness to your life in our frailty;
all this and more we bring.

**All for transformation through grace and love,
made known in Jesus Christ our Saviour.
Amen**

Donald Eadie

Go in peace (A poem at a healing service)

'Go in peace.
Your faith has made you whole.'

If you asked me why I am here,
What I expect,
How I understand healing,
For each and for all –
I would not know what to say.
But I would still be here,
With others, equally unsure,
With you, who share our pain.
All we offer is uncertainty:
Our night questions,
Our pain or fear or regret,
Our sighs and longings,
Our restless hearts,
Our emptiness and the emptiness of our world.
And somehow this is faith,
Reaching out to touch
Torn hands and a wounded side,
And straining to hear,
Beyond the questions, your word
That makes us well,
That makes all things well. [2]

Tony McClelland

Notes:

1. Used by permission of Inderjit Bhogal

2. Used by permission of Tony McClelland

Wild Goose Publications is part of the Iona Community:

- An ecumenical movement of men and women from different walks of life and different traditions in the Christian church
- Committed to the gospel of Jesus Christ, and to following where that leads, even into the unknown
- Engaged together, and with people of goodwill across the world, in acting, reflecting and praying for justice, peace and the integrity of creation
- Convinced that the inclusive community we seek must be embodied in the community we practise

Together with our staff, we are responsible for:

- Our islands residential centres of Iona Abbey, the MacLeod Centre on Iona, and Camas Adventure Centre on the Ross of Mull

and in Glasgow:

- The administration of the Community
- Our work with young people
- Our publishing house, Wild Goose Publications
- Our association in the revitalising of worship with the Wild Goose Resource Group

www.ionabooks.com

The Iona Community was founded in Glasgow in 1938 by George MacLeod, minister, visionary and prophetic witness for peace, in the context of the poverty and despair of the Depression. Its original task of rebuilding the monastic ruins of Iona Abbey became a sign of hopeful rebuilding of community in Scotland and beyond. Today, we are about 250 Members, mostly in Britain, and 1500 Associate Members, with 1400 Friends world-wide. Together and apart, 'we follow the light we have, and pray for more light'.

For information on the Iona Community contact:
The Iona Community, 21 Carlton Court,
Glasgow G5 9JP, UK. Phone: 0141 429 7281
e-mail: admin@iona.org.uk; web: www.iona.org.uk

For enquiries about visiting Iona, please contact:
Iona Abbey, Isle of Iona, Argyll PA76 6SN, UK. Phone: 01681 700404
e-mail: enquiries@iona.org.uk

Wild Goose Publications, the publishing house of the Iona Community established in the Celtic Christian tradition of Saint Columba, produces books, e-books, CDs and digital downloads on:

- holistic spirituality
- social justice
- political and peace issues
- healing
- innovative approaches to worship
- song in worship, including the work of the Wild Goose Resource Group
- material for meditation and reflection

For more information:

Wild Goose Publications
The Iona Community
21 Carlton Court, Glasgow, G5 9JP, UK

Tel. +44 (0)141 429 7281
e-mail: admin@ionabooks.com

or visit our website at
www.ionabooks.com
for details of all our products and online sales